AVP

AVP

Leading from the Unique Role of **Associate/Assistant Vice President** *for Student Affairs*

Editors **AMY HECHT** & **JASON B. PINA**

Foreword by **KEVIN KRUGER**

AVP: Leading from the Unique Role of Associate/Assistant Vice President for Student Affairs

Copyright © 2016 by the National Association of Student Personnel Administrators (NASPA), Inc. All rights reserved.

Published by

NASPA–Student Affairs Administrators in Higher Education
111 K Street, NE
10th Floor
Washington, DC 20002
www.naspa.org

No part of this publication may be reproduced, stored in a retrieval system, or transmitted in any form or by any means, now known or hereafter invented, including electronic, mechanical, photocopying, recording, scanning, information storage and retrieval, or otherwise, except as permitted under Section 107 or 108 of the 1976 United States Copyright Act, without the prior written permission of the Publisher.

Additional copies may be purchased by contacting the NASPA publications department at 202-265-7500 or visiting http://bookstore.naspa.org.

NASPA does not discriminate on the basis of race, color, national origin, religion, sex, age, gender identity, gender expression, affectional or sexual orientation, or disability in any of its policies, programs, and services.

Library of Congress Cataloging-in-Publication Data
Names: Hecht, Amy. | Pina, Jason B.
Title: AVP : leading from the unique role of associate/assistant vice
  president for student affairs / Amy Hecht and Jason B. Pina.
Description: Washington, DC : NASPA-Student Affairs Administrators in Higher
  Education, [2016]
Identifiers: LCCN 2015038529 | ISBN 9780931654848
Subjects: LCSH: Student affairs administrators--United States. | Student
  affairs services--United States--Administration.
Classification: LCC LB2342.92 .H44 2016 | DDC 378.1/97--dc23 LC record available at http://lccn.loc.gov/2015038529

Printed and bound in the United States of America

FIRST EDITION

Contents

Foreword ix
Preface xiii
The Authors xvii

1 What Does It Take To Be A Great AVP 1
  Amy Hecht
  Transactional Flaws 2
  AVP Competencies 5
  Expectations 10
  Conclusion 11
  References 12

2 I'm Hired, Now What? Succeeding in Your First Year as an AVP 13
  Ann Marie Klotz and Vijay Pendakur
  The Interview Process: Preparation and Negotiation 14
  Getting the Offer 16
  Finding Your Fit 18
  Making the Most of Your First 90 Days 20
  Managing Up and Managing Down 23
  Balancing Day-to-Day Responsibilities With Strategic Initiatives 26
  Redefining Professional Development as an AVP 29
  Wisdom from Vice Presidents for Student Affairs 31
  Conclusion 32
  References 33

3 Single- Versus
Multiple-AVP Structures   35
Jeanine A. Ward-Roof and Ashanti Hands

Why Structures Matter 36
AVP Models: Single Versus Multiple 37
Similarities and Differences 38
Challenges and Successes 41
Best Practices 48
Innovation Directions 51
Conclusion 53
References 55

4 Leadership and Strategic Planning:
A Blend of the Visionary and Practical   57
Nancy Crimmin and Pauline Dobrowski

Leadership Defined 58
Leading Distinctly From the Middle 59
Leadership as a Critical Competency 61
Strategic Planning 62
Managing Relationships and Building Partnerships 65
*Managing Relationships Within the
    Strategic Planning Process 71*
Leading and Managing 74
Conclusion 76
References 76

5 Navigating the Politics   79
Jeanna Mastrodicasa

Higher Education and Politics 80
Power 82
Conflict 82
Managing Conflict 83
Being Successful in the Political Realm 85
Case Study 87

Conclusion   88
References   89

6   Human Resource Management   91
Julie Payne-Kirchmeier

Importance of Supervision   93
Supervision and Management   94
Supervision Challenges for AVPs   95
Types and Models of Supervision   98
AVP Supervision and Management   102
Conclusion   116
References   117

7   Managing Fiscal Resources   119
Sean Stallings, Jason B. Pina, and Amy Hecht

Portfolio, Division, and Institutional
  Budget Process   122
Funding Sources and Management   123
Budget Models   127
Budget Development Cycle   130
Business Analysis: Cultivating Your Inner CEO   131
Conclusion   134
References   135

8   Beyond Balance: Developing Work–Life Integration   137
Jason B. Pina

Uniqueness of the AVP Role   139
Time Management   140
Prioritizing   143
Guiding Questions   146
Bringing It All Together   149
Conclusion   153
References   153

9 Maximizing the Role   155
   Cynthia Hernandez

   Maintaining Motivated AVPs 156
   Reasons for Remaining 157
   Remaining Effective 161
   Why We Do the Work 161
   Committing to Life-long Learning 165
   Maximizing the Role 168
   New Initiatives or Areas of Supervision 169
   Serving as the Interim 170
   Building Partnerships 171
   From Involvement to Engagement 172
   Conclusion 173
   References 173

10 Taking the Journey from AVP to VPSA   175
   Levester Johnson and Joan L. Kindle

   I Always Knew 177
   Don't Box Me In 180
   I Took a Wrong Turn 185
   I Stayed True to Myself 190
   I Was Called 195
   I Returned to the Water 198
   Conclusion 202

APPENDIX A: AVP Checklist for Success   207

APPENDIX B: AVP Self-Assessment   209

APPENDIX C: AVP Productivity Planner   213

Index   215

Foreword

> "In this lifetime we are like Superman who must remain disguised as the nerdy newspaper journalist Clark Kent, or Harry Potter and his friends who are not allowed to do magic while they are on holiday, away from Hogwarts School of Witchcraft and Wizardry… but even Harry Potter and Clark Kent get to tap into their 'special powers' once in a while, especially when the going gets tough."
>
> —Anthon St Maarten,
> *Divine Living: The Essential Guide To Your True Destiny*

The role of the associate/assistant vice president for student affairs (AVP) is much like the hero in a classic novel or award-winning movie. Strong yet compassionate, action-oriented one day and behind the scenes the next, a trusted confidant, the person who gets things done. Indeed, the AVP is a master of "special powers," who often must make miracles happen and create magic with constrained human and fiscal resources.

The AVP is both the best and the most challenging role in the modern division of student affairs. The AVP is given freedom to generate and implement new ideas, to create innovation, and to be a true leader while still maintaining daily contact with students. On the other hand, the role has expanded with a laundry list of conflicting and seemingly unmanageable challenges in areas that include the budget, equity and inclusion issues, supervision, program management, strategic planning, assessment, sexual and gender-based violence, crisis response, and more. Even Clark Kent or any of the Hogwarts would be overwhelmed by the diversity, intensity, and immediacy of the expectations.

Throughout the chapters of this book, readers will explore the AVP's many roles and challenges, presented in a well-written, engaging format. The authors examine the many hats worn by the AVP and the accompanying challenges. Those roles including the following:

Crisis Responder – The AVP is often at the center of an institutional response to crisis. Gun violence, sexual assault, protests on campus and in the local community, SARS, and the list goes on. The AVP plays a key role in threat assessment and working with care teams and behavioral intervention teams. Always on duty, the AVP is on speed dial to the campus police.

SSAO/VPSA Supporter – The AVP is the primary support professional for the vice president for student affairs (VPSA or senior student affairs officer), serving as both trusted confidant and advisor. The AVP keeps the VPSA informed of key campus climate issues and must translate VPSA leadership principles to fellow staff members. When the VPSA is misunderstood or actions result in student or staff disapproval, the AVP must straddle the line between translator of VPSA values and decisions and independent liaison maintaining the trust and respect of students and staff.

Visible Leader – The AVP must be visible. The successful AVP knows student leaders by name and regularly attends events, rallies, meetings, and campus activities. The AVP is often the student affairs staff representative at the dunking booth or flipping pancakes at the midnight Greek charity event. Only by embracing the "management by walking around" philosophy can an AVP identify hot spots and proactively manage emerging student affairs issues.

Fiscal Wizard – Doing more with less is the mantra of the modern AVP. Budget and staffing cuts are now the norm, and no immediate end is in sight to the fiscal crisis in higher education. As a result, the AVP is always searching for cost efficiencies and reductions. The AVP is a leader in exploring revenue alternatives, grants, intra-institutional partnerships, and new P3 (public–private partnerships) initiatives.

Strategic Planner and Thinker – The AVP puts the student affairs division strategic plan into action. Part planner and part implementer, the AVP must take a higher-level view of planning, and in some cases, must execute parts of the strategic plan. Finally, the AVP must motivate all staff to provide metrics and assessment data to measure progress toward strategic objectives.

Innovator – The AVP is the CIO—the chief innovation officer—for student affairs. The successful AVP builds on a solid professional network to discover exemplary and evidence-based practices that can be deployed on the home campus. The AVP understands the role of technology and social networking in communicating with students and developing new business services for students. Simultaneously, the AVP must be an incubator of new ideas and help create a culture of innovation.

Quiet Leader – The AVP must strike the right balance in calibrating the level of visible, public leadership that works best for the campus. Some institutions allow the AVP to take the spotlight, and others demand a more discrete role. The AVP must gauge when the VPSA, or even the college president, receives credit and when it is acceptable to share some of the sunshine. Generative and generous VPSAs eagerly give credit, but in other circumstances, AVPs must quietly take pride in their contributions to the overall mission of the institution.

The "buck" does not stop at the AVP desk, but it definitely passes through the AVP office. Most major decisions and issues that impact student affairs will land on the AVP desk and will require thoughtful analysis before briefing the VPSA and preparing for action.

Just as the role of student affairs has expanded in recent years, so has the role of the AVP at today's colleges and universities. For the new AVP searching for a road map, for the veteran AVP looking to re-energize efforts, or for the VPSA seeking to strengthen relationships with the AVP, this book is an invaluable resource—especially when the going gets tough.

Kevin Kruger
President
NASPA–Student Affairs Administrators in Higher Education

Preface

Regardless of the position they hold, student affairs professionals often have books on senior leadership lining their shelves. These books focus on the vice president position—what it takes to get there, what it takes to be successful in the role, and even how to advance beyond the vice presidency. The literature in student affairs is full of publications on the chief student affairs position. However, books on the associate/assistant vice president (AVP) position are nonexistent. Some could argue that these are also senior positions and that books on the vice presidency are relevant to those in AVP positions. But as AVPs we had difficulty finding a network and professional development resources to help us transition into the AVP role and be successful in the position.

When we first became AVPs for student affairs, we realized that although we had the credentials for the position, what had made us successful in previous roles would not necessarily make us successful as AVPs. As we searched for professional development opportunities, we were limited to books and conferences geared toward preparing us to become vice presidents. Although we wanted to eventually take on that role, we knew that we needed to first be great AVPs. A mentor connected Amy with Karen Warren Coleman, who at the time was an AVP at the University of Chicago. Amy and Karen bonded over their experiences as new AVPs and realized that if they were looking for a network, perhaps other AVPs were too.

After submitting a program proposal for the 2012 NASPA Annual Conference, Amy and Karen were connected by NASPA to two other

AVPs who had submitted a similar topic: Brandi Hephner LaBanc and Kelly Wesener Michael. At the time, both women were AVPs at Northern Illinois University. The four women hosted a panel discussion on the AVP role, which led to more roundtables and eventually to publishing an article titled "Developing the Next Generation of SSAOs" in the Spring 2012 issue of NASPA's *Leadership Exchange* magazine. In many ways the article, an overview of the numerous and diverse roles of AVPs, served as the foundation for this book.

As the need to develop and encourage AVPs became clearer, NASPA established the AVP Steering Committee in 2012. In the following 3 years a committed group of professionals sponsored regional and national programs, developed competencies, and advanced the concept of excellence in the AVP position. In addition to this work, NASPA sponsored an annual institute designed for new and experienced AVPs. This multiday event garnered rave reviews and expanded the support systems for AVPs across the country.

Although no AVP position or portfolio fits into a cookie-cutter design, the position has become increasingly common in organizations and provides an opportunity to influence organizations in a profound way. In addition, student affairs has become more complex with new initiatives and student demands as well as external pressure from compliance agencies and rising accountability. Many of these new responsibilities fall within the AVP's purview. As a consequence, the AVP role has proliferated on many campuses and garnered increased attention.

This book expands on the efforts made by NASPA and the committee by developing content relevant to AVPs. We hope it serves as a foundation for future publications and research focused on AVPs.

This book is designed to be read in two ways. First, it is laid out to be read straight through as the life cycle of the AVP. Chapters 1 and 2 offer fundamental research pertaining to excellence in the AVP role and outline the critical transition from candidate to successful AVP. Chapters 3 through 8 offer insight into a number of key components to successful AVP leadership. Chapters 9 and 10 outline two subjects that are particularly important when facing a career crossroads. Chapter 9 speaks to maximizing the AVP role and validates professionals who choose not to pursue a vice presidency. The concluding chapter speaks to those who desire the vice presidency and offers insights into making that professional decision. The second way this book can be used is as a reference for key topics and competencies an AVP may need to address from time to time. Because of the wide variance in AVP portfolios, some chapters are more relevant, depending on the issues at play on a particular campus.

At the end of this book readers will find three worksheets designed to help them in their professional journeys. The AVP Checklist for Success (see Appendix A) is referenced in Chapter 2 and can serve as a complement to the first 90 days as an AVP. The AVP Self-Assessment (see Appendix B) is based on the AVP competencies created in 2012 by NASPA's AVP Steering Committee and can identify areas for development. Julie Payne-Kirchmeier developed this assessment tool in 2014 to help individuals identify relative strengths and opportunities for growth within the AVP role. The AVP Productivity Planner (see Appendix C) was developed as a resource for AVPs to manage their workday. Amy Hecht developed the worksheet for this book to enable readers to incorporate key outcomes into their daily work, such as relationship building, strategic priorities, and work–life integration.

As members of NASPA's inaugural AVP Steering Committee and AVP Institute, we have grown personally from our involvement and observed first-hand the power of professional development at this level. This book is an effort to further advance excellence in the AVP role but also to expand the reach of the work undertaken in the last 3 years. Before and throughout the development of this project, the editors and authors found a dearth of research and published work related to student affairs AVPs. This book is not a definitive text on AVP excellence, but, rather, the beginning of a robust exchange among student affairs professionals.

November 2015 Amy Hecht
Ewing, New Jersey

Jason B. Pina
Bridgewater, Massachusetts

The Authors

Nancy Crimmin serves as the vice president for student affairs for Becker College. Previously she served as dean of campus life at Assumption College and has worked at Curry College and Alverno College. She received her bachelor's degree from Stonehill College, her master's degree in counseling and student personnel services from Springfield College, and her doctoral degree of education in educational leadership from Johnson and Wales University School of Education. Over the past 15 years, she has held numerous regional and national leadership positions within professional organizations, including NASPA, and she also serves as an adjunct faculty member at Springfield College, teaching in the student personnel master's program.

Pauline Dobrowski serves as the vice president for student affairs at Stonehill College. She earned her bachelor's degree from Boston College and her master's degree from Simmons College. She has served in higher education since 1994 at both Stonehill College and Wentworth Institute of Technology. In addition, she has held multiple regional and national leadership roles within various professional organizations, including NASPA.

Ashanti Hands serves as the dean of student affairs at San Diego Mesa College, one of the largest of California's 112 community colleges. Prior to joining the community college system in 2008, she served as dean of student affairs at the University of California, San Diego's Thurgood

Marshall College. As a senior student affairs officer, she has had administrative leadership and management of functional areas including student affairs, student equity, residential life, financial aid, student health services, outreach, student conduct, scholarship, and commencement. She earned her bachelor's degree in sociology from the University of California, San Diego, and her master's degree in education with an emphasis in multicultural counseling and doctoral degree in educational leadership from San Diego State University. She was one of the inaugural faculty members for the NASPA AVP Institute.

Amy Hecht serves as the vice president for student affairs at The College of New Jersey. She earned her bachelor's degree from Florida State University and her master's and doctoral degrees from the University of Pennsylvania. She has served in higher education since 2001 at Alpha Chi Omega Fraternity, the University of Pennsylvania, Cabrini College, Temple University, and Auburn University. She currently holds a faculty appointment at The College of New Jersey. She served as the inaugural chair of NASPA's AVP Steering Committee and the faculty director for the 2016 NASPA AVP Institute. Her areas of research interest include leadership development, organizational learning, and organizational development.

Cynthia Hernandez serves as the assistant vice president for student affairs at Texas A&M University. She has more than 19 years of experience in higher education and student affairs work. She earned her bachelor's degree in animal science and her master's degree in educational administration with an emphasis in student affairs administration, and a doctoral degree in educational administration from Texas A&M University. She is a member of several professional organizations, including the Association for Student Conduct Administration and the Association for Orientation, Transition, and Retention in

Higher Education (NODA), where she held the position of president. Hernandez serves as the chair of the NASPA AVP Steering Committee and is involved in many initiatives geared toward AVPs.

Levester Johnson, better known as "L.J." to colleagues and friends, serves as the vice president for student affairs at Butler University. He attended Marquette University where he earned his bachelor's degree in broadcast communications. He earned his master's degree in college student personnel at Southern Illinois University–Carbondale and his doctorate of education degree from Indiana University. He has held numerous leadership positions within higher education associations including NASPA, where he served as the first chair of the NASPA Board of Directors and was honored as a NASPA Pillar of the Profession. He has also been recognized throughout higher education for his approach to engaging campus communities through the use of social media.

Joan L. Kindle is vice chancellor for education and training at the Eastern Iowa Community College District. Her career in higher education administration spans three decades, including posts as associate provost, assistant to the president, vice president for student affairs, assistant vice president, and dean of student development. She has held several leadership roles within NASPA, including serving on the Board of Directors and the James E. Scott Academy Board, as well as serving as director of the 2015 NASPA Institute for New Vice Presidents for Student Affairs. She has received several Innovation Awards from the Illinois Council of Community College Administrators and the Exemplary Practices Award from the National Academic Advising Association. She has also received recognition from NASPA, including Pillar of the Profession and Community College Outstanding Professional. She received her master's degree from Bowling Green State University in Ohio and her doctorate from National Louis University in Illinois.

Ann Marie Klotz is the dean for campus life and chief student affairs officer on the Manhattan campus of the New York Institute of Technology. Previously, she spent 14 years working in housing and residence life at Oregon State University, DePaul University, Ball State University, and Albion College. She earned her bachelor's degree from Grand Valley State University (in political science) and two master's degrees from Michigan State University (student affairs) and DePaul University (women and gender studies). She earned her doctoral degree from DePaul University where she studied the career trajectory and leadership styles of 10 female university presidents. She has served in multiple regional and national roles for NASPA, most notably within the Women in Student Affairs Knowledge Community. She is the recent recipient of the ACPA Standing Committee for Women Research and Scholarship Award. Personal and research interests include women's career development, professional staff recruitment, development of online communities, personal branding, and first-generation college students.

Jeanna Mastrodicasa serves as the associate vice president for operations with the Institute of Food and Agricultural Sciences at the University of Florida. She earned her bachelor's degree and law degree from the University of Georgia, a master's degree from the University of Tennessee, and a doctoral degree from the University of Florida. She has been employed at the University of Florida since 1997, in both academic and student affairs, including nearly 8 years as assistant vice president for student affairs. She also served as an elected city commissioner in Gainesville from 2006–2012. Her areas of research interest include assessment, technology use, generations in the workplace, and land-grant university leadership.

Julie Payne-Kirchmeier, a native Texan, earned her bachelor's degree in genetics, her master's of education degree in student affairs administration in higher education from Texas A&M University–College Station, and her doctoral degree in educational leadership, administration, and foundations from Indiana State University. Most recently, she earned the designation of Certified Auxiliary Services Professional from the National Association of Campus Auxiliary Services (NACAS). She is a faculty member in the master's program in higher education at Northwestern University. She also serves in leadership roles in both NACAS and NASPA. Her research interests include feminism and women's issues in higher education, social media use in student affairs, and student affairs organizational management.

Vijay Pendakur serves as an associate vice president for student affairs at California State University–Fullerton. He served previously as director for the office of multicultural student success at DePaul University in Chicago. He is an experienced trainer and facilitator on issues of social justice and diversity education, and his primary research interests are Asian American college students, critical race theory, and college student retention and student success interventions. He holds a bachelor's degree in history and East Asian studies from the University of Wisconsin, Madison; a master's degree in U.S. history from the University of California, San Diego; and a doctorate in education from DePaul University. He is the editor of *Identity-Conscious Approaches to Student Success and Retention: Strategies to Close the Achievement Gap* (Stylus, 2016).

Jason B. Pina serves as the vice president for student affairs and enrollment management at Bridgewater State University. He earned a bachelor's degree in economics from Occidental College, his master's and educational specialist's degrees from the University of Northern Colorado, and a doctoral degree from Johnson & Wales University. He has served in higher education since 1994 at the University of Northern

Colorado, Babson College, Stonehill College, Roger Williams University, the University of Rhode Island, and Bridgewater State University. He has been an active member of NASPA in several regional and national capacities including Region I state director for Rhode Island, as well as serving on the inaugural AVP Steering Committee, James E. Scott Academy Board, and the ACPA/NASPA Professional Competencies Task Force. His research interests include diversity and social justice, presidential leadership, and leadership development.

Sean Stallings is an assistant vice president at The College of New Jersey, with more than 15 years of experience in higher education. He oversees residential education and housing, the student center, dining services, and the college bookstore and serves as a certified professional development trainer for the college's department of human resources. He earned his bachelor's and master's degrees from Rutgers University–New Brunswick and has completed all doctoral coursework in organizational leadership from Nova Southeastern University.

Jeanine A. Ward-Roof received her bachelor's degree in communications from Ohio University, master's degree in college student personnel from Bowling Green State University, and doctoral degree in educational leadership from Clemson University. She began her career in higher education at The University of Findlay, working in housing and activities, and after 2 years she moved to Clemson University where she worked with a number of functional areas during her 17-year tenure, including orientation, first-year programs, Greek life, and leadership. Additionally, she worked 7 years at Florida State University as dean of students, and in 2014 moved to serve as the vice president for student affairs at Ferris State University. She has been professionally involved by holding the role of president in the South Carolina College Personnel Association and NODA. She also served as treasurer and regional director for NASPA and has been the recipient of the NASPA Foundation Pillar of the Profession Award, NASPA Region III's Fred Turner Award, the NODA President's Award, and the NODA Outstanding Research Award. Her areas of research are orientation, parents and family members, and compassion fatigue.

What Does It Take To Be A Great AVP?

Amy Hecht

Little has been written about the associate/assistant vice president (AVP) role, the challenges it holds, and what success looks like in the position, yet it remains a coveted role. In fact, many professionals work years to advance their careers and obtain this position, which is extremely influential and has the potential to shape organizations. It only makes sense, therefore, to examine how AVPs can maximize their positions. This chapter introduces the concept of excellence in the AVP role and discusses the role's unique nature.

A variety of titles are used to describe this second-in-command position, including assistant or associate vice president, assistant or associate vice chancellor, dean of students, and assistant or associate dean of students. This book uses the term AVP to encompass the variety of titles that indicate a person reports to the vice president for student affairs (VPSA) and has senior oversight of departments and supports the macro goals of the senior leader.

Transactional Flaws

To get to the AVP role, professionals must have track records of success in previous positions, such as directorships. They have honed their administrative skills and been rewarded for being effective in these roles. Many have relied on these skills to advance their careers, and because they have been successful using that skill set, they often continue to operate in the same manner. This can be a fatal flaw for AVPs, because their new role requires a different, adapted skill set for success. For some, refusing to transition their skill set does not result in failure, but at a minimum AVPs are less than successful in their role if they don't adapt. For instance, an AVP who has been rewarded in previous roles for managing tasks and ensuring that objectives were achieved may be tempted to continue that behavior. Although that may ensure that certain objectives are met, it does not build a team's capacity or enable the AVP to lead and inspire others.

In their bestselling book, *What Got You Here, Won't Get You There*, Goldsmith and Reiter (2012) articulated the need for leaders to examine their approach and adapt as they are promoted. In fact, the authors noted that relying on the skills that brought success in previous roles may hinder success in the new position. AVPs should recognize approaches that may need to be adapted. Goldsmith and Reiter went on to identify the most common traits that prevent good leaders from becoming great—transactional flaws (see Table 1.1). Even top performers can be guilty of these behaviors and may experience success despite these transactional flaws. But the authors argued that those who are willing to examine themselves and make behavioral changes can be even more successful.

Table 1.1. Traits That Keep Good Leaders from Being Great

Transactional Flaw	Description
Winning too much	The need to win at all costs and in all situations—when it matters, when it doesn't, and when it's totally beside the point.
Adding too much value	The overwhelming desire to add our two cents to every discussion.
Passing judgment	The need to rate others and impose our standards on them.
Making destructive comments	The needless sarcasms and cutting remarks that we think make us sound sharp and witty.
Starting with "no," "but," or "however"	The overuse of these negative qualifiers, which secretly say to everyone, "I'm right. You're wrong."
Telling the world how smart we are	The need to show people we're smarter than they think we are.
Speaking when angry	Using emotional volatility as a management tool.
Negativity, or "Let me explain why that won't work"	The need to share our negative thoughts even when we aren't asked.
Withholding information	The refusal to share information in order to maintain an advantage over others.
Failing to give proper recognition	The inability to praise and reward.
Claiming credit that we don't deserve	The most annoying way to overestimate our contribution to any success.
Making excuses	The need to reposition our annoying behavior as a permanent fixture so people excuse us for it.
Clinging to the past	The need to deflect blame away from ourselves and onto events and people from our past; a subset of blaming others.
Playing favorites	Failing to see that we are treating someone unfairly.
Refusing to express regret	The inability to take responsibility for our actions, admit we're wrong, or recognize how our actions affect others.
Not listening	The most passive-aggressive form of disrespect for colleagues.
Failing to express gratitude	The most basic form of bad manners.
Punishing the messenger	The misguided need to attack the innocent who are usually only trying to help us.

Transactional Flaw	Description
Passing the buck	The need to blame everyone but ourselves.
An excessive need to be "me"	Exalting our faults as virtues simply because they're who we are.

Note. Adapted from *What Got You Here Won't Get You There: How Successful People Become Even More Successful!* by M. Goldsmith and M. Reiter, 2012, pp. 40–41, New York, NY: Hyperion. Reprinted with permission.

Some AVPs rely on skills or exhibit traits from the past that do not serve them well in their new role. For instance, an AVP could have developed self-promoting traits in a previous position where he or she was rewarded for telling others about accomplishments. This trait, referred to by Goldsmith and Reiter (2012) as "winning too much," could be harmful and might prevent the individual from excelling in the AVP role. Recognizing those traits or skills that do not serve you well in the AVP position can move you toward excellence in the role. At the same time, AVPs should analyze the traits that do serve them well or refocus their strengths in a new direction. For instance, in the previous example, the "winning too much" trait could be used to communicate your direct reports' successes and celebrate what they are accomplishing. Identifying and refocusing possible transactional flaws require thoughtful self-reflection and an evaluation of the organization's culture. The self-assessment should take into consideration the VPSA's expectations and the needs of the portfolio.

Each AVP role is unique, composed of a variety of departments and areas of responsibilities. At times, AVPs have direct experience in some areas, but it is more likely that they supervise and lead departments in which they have had limited experience. Those new to their roles may feel the pressure to learn as much as possible about these areas, but that is not always necessary. AVPs should have a broad enough understanding to be able to support their units, but having a strong unit leader (often a director) with the required expertise is more important. Having the confidence to learn from direct reports and identify how you can advance strategic goals should be the focus for AVPs.

Depending on the size and structure of the organization, there may also be more than one AVP in any given organization. Single- versus multiple-AVP models influence the role. The organizational structure affects the way work is accomplished and how information is communicated. Chapter 3 discusses these organizational structures and provides guidance on how to navigate them, but be aware that this nuance influences the role of an AVP.

AVP Competencies

Although each AVP role offers a different set of challenges, many commonalities occur across these positions. In 2013, NASPA's AVP Steering Committee identified a set of core competencies that are relevant across all types of AVP roles. These competencies were developed using feedback during the 2013 AVP preconference session (as part of the NASPA Annual Conference), a 2013 survey of AVPs, NASPA regional conference roundtables, the 2013 Richard F. Stevens Institute, and a review of the *Professional Competency Areas for Student Affairs Practitioners* (American College Personnel Association & NASPA, 2010). These AVP competencies form the foundation of excellence in the AVP role (see Table 1.2). Each competency was divided into levels: transitioning, navigating, and leading. In the section that follows, each competency is identified according to these levels.

Table 1.2. AVP Competencies

Competency	Definition
Politics	Establishing important relationships and navigating the political arena of the institution and community.
Position skills	Developing the basic competencies necessary to perform the AVP role.
Human resource management	Understanding team dynamics, professional or staff development, and development of appropriate staffing structures supportive of the student affairs' vision.
Leadership and strategic vision	Understanding full culture and environment of the institution, the role student affairs plays within the environment, change management, and the long-term direction of student affairs.
Resource allocation, acquisition, and management	Continually identifying ways to attract, align, and maximize resources within the division.
Strategic assessment and evaluation	Understanding the development of outcomes, creating and implementing assessment protocols, and interpreting data for use long-range planning.
Law and policy	Understanding the most current public policy, legislative changes, and legal decisions impacting higher education; developing student affairs practices that adhere to policy and law.

Politics

Politics is one of the more complex components of the AVP role. Many professionals in student affairs shy away from the term *political* to describe their actions because of negative connotations. However, if you reframe politics as relationships, you can view this competency as a means to advance work that ultimately benefits students. As professionals new to the role at the transitioning level, AVPs should identify key stakeholders; as they navigate this competency, they should build relationships; and, finally, as they lead within this competency, they should build partnerships that benefit the division's strategic direction.

As a representative of the VPSA, AVPs often feel as though they are in the middle and unsure of how to approach politics on campus. Supporting the VPSA while developing your own political capital requires a delicate balance; you don't want your efforts to overshadow the VPSA.

The AVP plays a significant role in building bridges across campus, developing essential relationships with partners and enabling the division to achieve its goals and objectives. Successfully navigating and embracing the political nature of higher education institutions leads to success in the number two position and beyond. This topic is more fully explored in Chapter 5.

Position Skills

Position skills are those required to operate as an AVP; they include expertise in particular software or processes that an institution uses, communication techniques, or the ability to analyze data and make critical resource decisions.

One particular skill set to highlight is managing up, down, and across the organization. Managing up involves creating the results that the VPSA is looking for and communicating those effectively (Sturt & Nordstrom, 2014). Understanding the needs of supervisors, what they value, and what will make them look good are all components of managing up. Managing down involves building and supporting your team (Sturt & Nordstrom, 2014). As a supervisor, how do you remove barriers so that your star performers can excel? How do you celebrate success? How do you communicate strategic direction and frame opportunities? Managing across the organization involves building strong relationships with your peers and being a team player. These relationships should not be ignored; not only do they allow an AVP to be more effective, VPSAs expect their teams to work together effectively, so this component is also a part of managing up.

As AVPs transition, they become aware of the skills they need for the new role; as they navigate the position, they incorporate these skills into their work; and, finally, those who lead in this area can teach others how to effectively represent the VPSA in their absence.

Human Resources Management

Excellence in the role includes the ability to effectively manage people, create organizational structures, and develop individuals to accomplish strategic goals. AVPs must think strategically about the structure of their portfolios while taking into consideration the greater student affairs organization. As AVPs advance in this competency area, they should move toward a collaborative role with the VPSA, making strategic human resource decisions that benefit the broader division.

Human resource management at the AVP level is complex and requires both management and leadership skills. AVPs are asked to consider institutional, divisional, and portfolio perspectives in decision making. This can complicate the management and advocacy for human resources. An AVP must advocate for their portfolio, but at the same time balance the needs of the larger organization. Chapter 6 focuses on human resource management as an AVP and provides guidance for navigating this competency.

Leadership and Strategic Vision

As AVPs transition into the role, they should understand the strategic direction of the organization; as they navigate the role, they represent this direction in their work across the division; and as AVPs lead in the role, they represent the strategic direction externally through their work with stakeholders both inside and outside the institution. Chapter 4 discusses this competency.

AVPs need to flex between day-to-day management and institutional or divisional leadership. The challenge for AVPs in this area is to represent the VPSA's vision but also interpret it for their areas. Again, an AVP is left balancing between representing the VPSA's vision and reflecting that vision in leadership efforts.

Resource Allocation, Acquisition, and Management

The unique nature of the AVP role requires a broad understanding of various funding sources, the ability to align financial resources with division priorities, and the skills to communicate and advocate for those resources. Most AVPs have had extensive budgeting experience prior to assuming the role, but AVPs manage more complex resources, which requires a broad understanding of the institution and the priorities of the VPSA. As AVPs transition into their role, they should make it a priority to learn the budget system, funding sources, and processes for acquiring new resources (such as the grant process). As AVPs move from transitioning to navigating, they should build the relationships necessary to secure resources; and as they lead within this competency, they should build a track record of successfully securing resources for strategic initiatives. Chapter 7 dives deeper into managing fiscal resources.

Strategic Assessment and Evaluation

AVPs are often responsible for pulling assessment data and communicating meaning both within the division and beyond. To do this successfully, AVPs must have a broad understanding of research methods and the ability to think critically about the impact of data. Although this book does not explore assessment and evaluation, a number of resources are available in the literature and within professional development opportunities to support development within this competency.

Law and Policy

The AVP Steering Committee identified an understanding of current laws and policies as a critical competency for AVPs. In the current environment, AVPs often must interpret and implement federal requirements and state laws. The ability to learn quickly, manage complexity, and build the relationships to fulfill those legal mandates is a requirement of those in these positions. This is an ongoing process and remaining relevant should be a top priority for AVPs.

Most AVPs enter the role with at least a basic understanding of the laws that affect student affairs. As AVPs move on to navigating this competency, they need to communicate across the division the implications of legislation. Finally, as they start to lead, AVPs should understand the broader impact of laws and policies across the institution and anticipate the role student affairs needs to play in complying with requirements. Although this book does not address the law and policy competency, numerous resources, such as conferences, webinars, and journal articles, address this area.

Overall, the core competencies are flexibility and the ability to manage multiple responsibilities, many of which are high-profile initiatives for the organization. The challenge is balance. AVPs describe their position as having one foot in the role of strategic, divisionwide leader and the other in a manager or support position to the VPSA. This role is unique and requires professionals who can adapt and flex their style—going from strategic visionary to someone implementing policy behind the scenes.

Expectations

Many AVPs wonder what is expected of their position and how best to support their VPSAs. Each VPSA is unique, coming to the position with different expectations. Additionally, institutions often have a unique culture and organization that require VPSAs to structure their responsibilities and their own role in different ways, which results in the diversity of roles and duties that AVPs have. AVPs should find the time to talk with their VPSAs to clarify expectations.

At the 2015 NASPA AVP Institute, current VPSAs shared their perspectives on what they need from their AVPs. VPSAs spoke about the need for their AVPs to support them. One referred to this as "having my back." VPSAs need a level of trust with the AVPs and assurance that they are working together to advance the division, but AVPs should also help the VPSA be successful. AVPs provide appropriate feedback to the VPSAs, represent them in their absence, and take important projects off the VPSA's plate. VPSAs need an AVP that makes them look good.

Second, the VPSAs noted that AVPs should be able to handle challenges in their areas without the involvement of the VPSA. At the same time, AVPs should know what to communicate to their supervisors and when. Finding the balance of keeping a VPSA in the loop and handling challenges personally is important. Finally, the VPSAs shared that they need an AVP who can get things done. Whether it's creating new programs, building partnerships, or responding to new federal legislation, AVPs need to learn quickly and successfully take on the task at hand.

Conclusion

The AVP role has become increasingly common in student affairs organizations and has the potential to influence both the division and the greater institution. Understanding the nuances of this position and committing to the pursuit of excellence within the role are essential. As more student affairs professionals advance into the AVP role, understanding the position and what success looks like is paramount. This chapter provides a framework for AVPs to assess strengths and make adaptations based on the requirements of the new position. The self-assessment should not end here but become an ongoing reflective process throughout your career.

References

American College Personnel Association and National Association of Student Personnel Administrators. (2010). *Professional competency areas for student affairs practitioners.* Retrieved from https://www.naspa.org/images/uploads/main/Professional_Competencies.pdf

Goldsmith, M., & Reiter, M. (2012). *What got you here won't get you there: How successful people become even more successful!* New York, NY: Hyperion.

Sturt, D., & Nordstrom, T. (2014). Managing up or down? What are you being graded on? [Blog post]. *Forbes.* Retrieved from http://www.forbes.com/sites/davidsturt/2014/04/15/managing-up-or-down-what-are-you-being-graded-on

I'm Hired, Now What?
Succeeding in Your First Year as an AVP

Ann Marie Klotz and Vijay Pendakur

The associate/assistant vice president (AVP) role is often called the unsung hero of student affairs. AVPs are essential but misunderstood. They are not the vice president for student affairs (VPSA), but they also are no longer considered content-specific experts. Their work is often behind the scenes, managing strategic objectives for their vice presidents or coaching directors to rise up and deliver excellence in the face of new challenges. Although the arc of an AVP career can span a number of years, this chapter is about the start of the journey: the ever-so-important first year.

We are intimately familiar with the first year of the AVP journey, because both of us are currently new AVPs! Throughout this chapter, we share our expertise gleaned from our lived experience as student affairs professionals and the wisdom acquired from mentors, sponsors, conferences, and reading. Although we use one scholarly voice throughout this chapter, we offer the richness of our diverse experiences as AVPs. Ann Marie is currently the dean of campus life at the Manhattan campus of the New York Institute of Technology, a mid-sized, urban, private, STEM-focused, East Coast institution. Vijay is an associate vice president at California State University–Fullerton, a large, comprehensive, access-focused, public, West Coast institution. Both of us were hired as external candidates.

In this chapter, we cover several core focus areas that are critical to an AVP's success in the first year on the job: the interview process, negotiation, and pre-hiring preparatory work; navigating the first 90 days; managing up and managing down; balancing day-to-day responsibilities with strategic objectives; and redefining professional development as an AVP. Because the AVP role is so intimately tied to a vice president's vision and goals, we also conducted a small survey of 18 sitting vice presidents on how an AVP can be successful in the first year and we include a few of their key points later on. Finally, we end the chapter with a brief list of resources that are particularly useful in this major career transition.

The Interview Process: Preparation and Negotiation

Success in the AVP role can actually begin during the search and interview process. Each job search looks dramatically different, depending on whether it is an internal process or one conducted by an external search firm. A typical internal search is a multilevel process that involves many campus stakeholders. Often it includes multiple phone or Skype interviews and one or more campus interviews. References may be contacted at any point in the process but often are contacted prior to a campus visit. The identity of all finalists may be made public prior to the on-campus interview stage and should be anticipated from the time of application. The open-forum interview may be listed on the university website and published through any number of streaming entities. Ask the search chair or human resources to outline the process, including the timeline for reference checks and when the names of the finalists will be made public.

Preparation for these interviews should include careful study of the organizational chart, including direct reports, and reading the most recent divisional end-of-year report and university strategic plan. If possible, you may want to ask for a general budget for the position. Websites for private institutions allow you to examine IRS 990 filings. State institutions are at times subject to public disclosure and Freedom of Information Act disclosures that provide valuable data.

AVP searches are often managed by executive search firms that help institutions gather the best candidates and coordinate specific phases of the interviewing and vetting process. We have found that firm-run searches present different challenges than searches being run by the institution. The following story captures some of what Vijay learned as he navigated firm-run searches.

> In the year I spent searching for an AVP role, I thought I had figured out how the game works after being a candidate in a few searches. Then I saw a position I was really interested in, but the job description directed all interested applicants to submit their materials to a search firm, rather than applying directly to the institution's human resources website. So I worked on my cover letter and résumé and e-mailed them to the firm. Several weeks went by and I didn't hear anything. I was surprised, because I felt like my qualifications really lined up well with what the job description called for. I remember calling a mentor and asking if she

knew anything about the hiring institution's process and where they might be in the search timeline. My mentor asked me what I'd done with my application materials, and I told her that I'd e-mailed them to the search firm. She chuckled and kindly walked me through how I'd blown the first step in the process.

I learned that the firm represents the first "gateway" that you have to cross in a firm-run search process. They don't simply gather applications; they are screening for talent and trying to assemble a competitive pool for the hiring institution. I learned that it is important to have someone who is highly respected in our field "nominate" you with a firm, which entails them e-mailing the search manager at the firm with a note about you that describes why you'd be a good fit for the role. A nomination usually results in the firm reaching out to you for an "informational conversation," which is actually a mini-interview, so it is critical to do your homework and impress the recruiter during this conversation. After the informational conversation, the recruiter might ask you to submit your materials, and that's when you can send in your cover letter and résumé. Unfortunately, it was too late for me to follow this process for the position that had caught my eye. Happily, when my current institution launched their AVP search and enlisted a firm to help them with the process, I knew just how to manage the process and here I am in my first AVP role!

Getting the Offer

Once you have the offer, thinking about the next steps can be overwhelming. A few areas to consider when contemplating questions and requests during the job search process:

Is the salary competitive? The College and University Professional Association for Human Resources releases survey data each year to share the salary range of different roles in student affairs based on institutional type (see the 2013–2014 list at https://www.higheredjobs.com/Salary/salaryDisplay.cfm?SurveyID=26).

What is the cost of living conversion? This is an important question to consider. Prior to accepting an on-campus interview, consider the difference between where you are now and where you are potentially going. If the cost of living is higher, find out whether the higher salary actually increases the take-home compensation. CNN offers an easy-to-understand cost-of-living calculator (http://money.cnn.com/calculator/pf/cost-of-living).

Is the benefits package comparable to or better than what you currently receive? Ask for this information when offered the on-campus interview. Review this information carefully and ask the human resources representative more detailed questions about benefits prior to accepting the position.

How does the retirement program work? Find out when the university begins contributing. Ann Marie was told that every employee must wait 1 year to be vested in the university's 401(k) program. She asked the VPSA to advocate for the university to waive the requirement, and it did. Always ask!

What does the institution offer for relocation? According to several search firms, 5% of the yearly salary is commonly offered to relocate. If you are offered $100,000 per year, ask for $5,000 in relocation funds. Once you have accepted the on-campus offer, get a few moving estimates and be prepared to negotiate for what you need. Typically, estimates are good for 30 to 60 days, so being proactive in this process can eliminate the stress of getting estimates while trying to manage everything else in the transition.

What about partner employer assistance programs, local child care, realtors, and schools? Even if these items do not apply to your situation today, it may help shape your leadership around team development and recruiting. Other amenities to consider: meal plan, parking space, technology (e.g., laptop, mobile devices, phone, etc.), professional development funds, and temporary housing.

Finding Your Fit

In searching for a new student affairs position, "fit" is one of the most difficult qualities to define and one of the most important determinants of a new hire's success in the role. When considering the AVP role, determine whether your skill set and values align with what you are expected to do. Institutional culture affects all facets of leadership, and it is important to have a good understanding of the work culture, the ethos around change, and the level of autonomy you will have within this position.

In order to determine fit, consider several areas. A large determinant of your success in this role is about the relationship, or fit, that you will have with your vice president. Do your homework to find out more about your potential supervisor. At the on-campus interview, Ann Marie's vice president gave her the names of five people who had worked for him in previous roles and encouraged her to contact them to find out how he operated in the workplace and with his direct reports. Consider which questions you want to ask the VPSA in order to gain a better understanding of his or her goals and perspective.

- What qualities are essential for the person to succeed in this role?
- What would success look like in this role 1 year from now?
- What kind of help do you need in this role to carry out your vision for the division?
- What are the current budgetary realities of the division and university?
- What is not in the job description that you need the successful candidate to know or do?

If you are an internal candidate, some of these questions may be slightly different, because you may have additional knowledge of the role and the

VPSA. Consider discussing how you would transition into this role and what kind of support you may need from peers and other campus stakeholders in this new position.

Try to determine the top three priorities for this role (as outlined by your supervisor and mentioned by the staff in the interview). Are they areas that speak to your skill set? Do they excite you? Additionally, what kind of AVP are you being asked to be? Do they need a fixer, a change maker, someone to continue the work of the previous AVP? Often different groups want different things. What your supervisor asks for may differ from what students, staff, and faculty ask for. Do you find any commonalities between what campus stakeholders are asking for in this interview process? Once you find the answers to these questions, you need to decide whether the description matches the kind of AVP you can and want to be.

When Ann Marie interviewed for her current job, the VPSA charged her to "do and create big things" on campus. He wanted her to not be afraid to be bold, to innovate, and to cultivate real change. More important, he affirmed that he would support her publicly and privately in doing so. This was the kind of position that fit her skills and professional desires, but it is not a fit for everyone.

Alternately, Vijay's VPSA was searching for an AVP to work on several retention and graduation aspects of the institutional strategic plan. Aside from the general management and leadership skill sets common to an AVP role, the VPSA was searching for a practitioner with a depth of knowledge in one niche to help with the university's ambitious student success agenda. This was a great fit for Vijay, but it might not have been the right AVP role for other candidates. Know the kind of AVP the institution is asking for and determine whether there is role congruence.

Making the Most of Your First 90 Days

Across a number of industries, ranging from higher education to large corporations, the first 90 days in a new leadership role are thought of as critical, fertile ground for a leader's long-term success in the role (Watkins, 2003). In the first few months as a new AVP, you have three key priorities: Understand the needs and vision of your supervisor, learn the short- and long-term priorities that define your role, and discover the political and structural realities of the institution. A new AVP's ability to quickly and accurately ascertain these varying opportunities and constraints profoundly shapes the success in this role.

The AVP is a key support person for the VPSA at any institution. Thus, the success of AVPs is often tied directly to their ability to understand their supervisor's needs and vision for the division and the institution. Within the first few supervisory meetings, new AVPs should ask their supervisors to explicitly name what kind of support they are looking for and the priorities that they can begin to address, thereby bolstering the VPSA's vision and outcomes. We recommend that you ask your VPSA about any current political or budgetary "hot issues" that can help you understand the current context of your institution. If you submit a regular report to your supervisor, consider structuring your report to match your supervisor's stated priorities and needs. This effort not only helps you track your work, time management, and accomplishments over time, but it also empowers your supervisor to understand your contributions to the institution in a way he or she already values.

Beyond structuring communication with your supervisor, consider how you message your supervisor's vision to stakeholders inside and outside your division. As the number two, you often have the opportunity to shape or extend a shared narrative with stakeholders. Part of supporting your VPSA is understanding the messages he or she is trying to disseminate so you can mirror these in your spheres of influence. Finally, it is critical for you to gain your supervisor's trust in the first 90 days and demonstrate that you are communicating a shared vision and narrative.

Being an AVP is an active process of trust building, good judgment, and proactive communication that allows you to be the number two in your VPSA's eyes. In your first 3 months as an AVP, consider how you can bring your VPSA not just problems, but potential solutions, or how you can share what you are hearing across campus to alert the VPSA to a possible challenge. These actions go far in building trust, which will enable your supervisor to further lean on you to support his or her vision and priorities. Note that your ability to build trust depends on a number of factors, including your supervisor's tenure in the role, length of time at the institution, relationship with his or her supervisor, and reputation among peers.

The first 3 months as an AVP are not just a time to be "looking up" to learn about your supervisor's vision and priorities. These crucial months are a time for you to gather valuable data and context to develop your own priorities and a vision for your work in the first year. Most AVP roles come with a portfolio of departments or service units to manage. We suggest conducting a review of these units to assess what they do, how they manage their talent and their budgets, and how they shape the student learning experience. We advise conducting this review in a nonthreatening manner, because your new supervisees might be nervous about your arrival; the idea of a "review" might produce anxiety. An unobtrusive review might include reading through the previous year's annual reports for your departments, asking a similar set of questions to each of your directors in your first few supervisory meetings, or asking cross-campus stakeholders to share their thoughts with you on how your units are doing. It can also be helpful to obtain the résumés of all direct reports to learn more about their experiences and consider how they can contribute to the divisional goals in a variety of ways. By the end of your first 90 days, a thoughtful review process enables you to develop a set of priorities and goals to guide your work with your portfolio in your first year or two.

Finally, we cannot overemphasize the importance of thoroughly investigating the political and budgetary realities of your institution in your first 3 months on the job. These contexts either serve as the foundation for your success or, if you do not understand them well, become insurmountable barriers to your effective leadership and change management. We suggest that you gather contextual data through both formal and informal avenues.

First, read your institutional and divisional strategic plans carefully. Understand how key documents were constructed; look into the vision, culture, and previous leadership that shaped them. These documents should also demonstrate how the AVP job description was created. How do the duties of the role support the stated divisional and university goals? Study any documents that discuss the mission of your institution or the vision of your executive leadership. Ask your divisional budget expert to walk you through the budgets for all the departments in your portfolio and ask lots of questions along the way.

These formal methods of learning help you understand certain aspects of your institution's political and budgetary contexts. In addition to these efforts, ask your VPSA for a list of key "context experts" inside and outside your division. These are often staff, faculty, and administrators who have been at the institution for quite some time (or are strategically positioned within the new administrative regime) and serve as repositories of stories and information that can be just as valuable as the formal contextual data. In your first 90 days, find a way to meet with every one of these context experts and listen, listen, listen.

Managing Up and Managing Down

The role of an AVP is about maintaining a critical balance of support and advocacy for your direct reports while working to advance your VPSA's agenda. In this role you have to filter the needs, wants, and frustrations of your direct reports up—when appropriate—while simultaneously determining what you can take off the plate of your supervisor. It is a tricky balancing act and one that requires excellent discernment skills.

It is critical to determine what you can manage and what needs to be pushed up the chain of command. Most of what you encounter in this role on a daily basis can and should be managed by you (Watkins, 2003). This is a marked difference from lower level positions where the typical mantra has been to *pass it up* when there is an issue. In this role, you are asked to manage much of what comes your way, because the VPSA is managing much of what has been *passed down*.

Because you are viewed as a direct link to the VPSA, many colleagues may seek your counsel and advice when they disagree with something that is happening within the division. This is where a combination of being accessible, listening, and helping people create strategies to solve their challenges is most important. A big part of your job is to manage the day-to-day operations of the division while the VPSA is representing student affairs to the larger university community. Build trust with your supervisor and demonstrate loyalty so your supervisor knows that you are responding to complaints or questions about his or her leadership appropriately. In the beginning, ask your supervisor how or whether he or she prefers to know about questions or complaints from other staff members. Your supervisor may direct you to manage and handle them or may opt to have you pass them up. Either way, knowing how to respond to these kinds of situations ensures you are both on the same page.

During your first year, create the foundation for communication up and down the organizational chart in order to foster positive working relationships and a culture where people feel valued and heard. The introduction of a new senior leader can create a shift in your institutional culture, especially for those in professional positions below the AVP. This change may lead to people feeling threatened or unsettled with the evolving organizational culture.

As you begin to meet with direct reports, staff members might call your attention to what they consider extremely urgent issues. They may be testing you to see on which things you jump and take action. Beware of alarmists. Use this time to take inventory of all perceived issues and concerns, but do not instantly make every crisis your top priority. Doing so can set a precedent whereby people expect you to act on everything they think is urgent, even if it is not.

Staff members may test boundaries by asking (covertly or overtly) what you think about other people in the organization (up to and including your VPSA and president). Regardless of your personal feelings, keep all communication about university personnel positive and professional. One less-than-flattering comment can be perceived (and repeated) as your not liking or not supporting someone, and this has no upside for you as a new AVP.

The following are suggestions for managing up:

- During your first few meetings with your VPSA, ask how much he or she wants to be copied on issues that involve your direct reports. Are there certain hot-button issues the VPSA wants to know about?
- Ask how your VPSA prefers to communicate. Does the VPSA desire phone calls instead of text messages? Are in-person updates adequate, or is a paper trail via e-mail preferred?
- Ask about the general performance concerning each of your direct reports and determine the areas of concern and improvement.

- Ask about the relationship between the VPSA and the president. Get an understanding of how the VPSA prefers that you handle issues that reach the president's office and the press.

When managing down, consider the following:

- Share your preferred communication patterns with your direct reports. For example, if you oversee housing and residence life, how do you want to be contacted after hours during a serious student issue? Let your staff know your expectations regarding communication and be sure to follow up if those guidelines are not followed.
- Develop a plan for meeting with your staff. Determine how often one-on-one meetings are needed and how you want to spend that time. Some AVPs prefer that their direct reports bring an agenda; others like that time to be more organic.
- Take responsibility for decisions even when they aren't yours. Part of your role is to support your VPSA's decisions and to disseminate that information to indicate that the leadership team supports it. People easily fall into a pattern of blaming the VPSA. Try to show by words and actions that decisions are made as a team.
- Learn about the budgets of each area and how money has typically been spent. In order to advocate for increased resources (including additional staffing), you have to develop a good understanding about where the money is going and how those spending patterns support the goals of the division and the university.

At times, you may experience information overload. You are charged with understanding the needs, priorities, and goals of the division while supporting individual staff and departmental initiatives. You may also be learning about a new institutional culture and a new supervisor. In order to manage these competing priorities, be mindful that setting expectations about communication goes a long way in helping you to be successful.

Balancing Day-to-Day Responsibilities With Strategic Initiatives

One of the challenges for new AVPs is balancing day-to day responsibilities with broader strategic initiatives their VPSAs want them to manage. One simple, but important, investment of your time and effort is how you position your administrative assistant, which depends on the institution and the setup of support staff. In some instances, multiple AVPs may share one administrative assistant, while at other institutions, the AVP has a dedicated support staff. During your on-campus interview, ask about the kind of administrative assistance that is available and learn more about how this person is expected to support you in this role.

Assistants can do so much more than manage your calendar and help you with paperwork. They can be your weekly time and energy manager if you empower them to do so. Each week, your assistant can help you look at your previous week and your upcoming week and think through how your time and energy is being spent. They can point out where you are overinvested and where you might need to spend more energy. They can also help you strike a better balance in caring for your personal needs with snack breaks, lunch times, and unscheduled time at your desk. But, for assistants to help you, they have to understand your short- and long-term strategic projects, as well as your day-to-day responsibilities. Educating and developing your assistant takes time and requires a strong working relationship, but doing so can help you immensely, because the empowered assistant can be a keen steward of your time and energy and a frequent source of accountability in a hectic professional role.

As you build trust, your VPSA might start giving you more and more strategic projects. Some of these projects might be multi-year transformative initiatives that require you to work hard for quite some time before your results are evident to the campus community. Therefore, it can be helpful to identify low-hanging fruit to pluck in your first year. Look for a department that has a simple budget or staffing issue that you can address, or try to alleviate a space issue by advocating for a department with your divisional leadership team. Perhaps you can partner with a group of students who have never had a listening ear in the upper administration. These small investments of your time can yield early wins that help reassure your campus community that they picked the right AVP.

Time management is an important skill in the role of an AVP. Determine early how you want to spend your time (e.g., meetings, office time, relationship building). Although unexpected situations may derail this plan on any given day, it is good to have a strategy as to how you approach daily tasks, long-term projects, and meetings.

Your days will be filled with meetings, if you let them. Ann Marie developed a unique time management strategy to navigate all of the competing demands of her job. The following is her account of how she avoided "death by meetings."

> Because I have a large number of direct reports, I quickly ascertained that the way to ensure consistent communication and to balance the heavy workload was to reframe the traditional notion of meetings. Each quarter, I schedule a one-on-one meeting with each of my direct reports. Besides those meetings, they drop by my office, call or text me, or ask for 15-minute appointments when they have questions. All seasoned professionals I supervise (directors and assistant or associate deans) have at least 10 years of experience in the field, so their needs are different from those of entry-level staff.
>
> We also meet as a campus-life team once per month (as opposed to weekly). They are in my office often and we connect frequently. I feel like we get

more done because they aren't waiting for a specific time once a week to get their questions answered. The staff report that they appreciate this style because it enables us to accomplish more in the course of a day. We are doing the work in real time and it feels consistent, efficient, and effective.

Finally, the general lesson for all AVPs is to examine your organization and assess the needs and priorities of the role and of your team. Create a strategy that works for your style and creates buy-in for the staff. Be open to tweaking this as needs emerge and evolve.

A second tactic for managing complex, strategic initiatives for your supervisor is saying no with grace. Take time to think through your supervisor's expectations of how you spend your time and energy. Those expectations should be the primary guide on when to say yes and when to say no. Remember also to give yourself space in the first year to really focus on learning the AVP role and campus from a new viewpoint. Creating the space to learn, reflect, and decompress takes time in your weekly schedule. Saying no to a few new opportunities and projects might feel like a setback, but it is a savvy investment in your first year as an AVP. When asked to add something else to your plate, consider the following questions:

- Does this opportunity advance the goals of my supervisor, division, or students?
- Am I the only person who can be tapped for this? Could this be delegated to a member of my staff?
- Can I say no to this now and perhaps get involved next year?

Although anything can be phrased as a priority for the university, only you can decide to which priorities you must dedicate time and effort.

We believe that your first year as an AVP can be the right time to think about how your portfolio is organized. Assess whether this is the best model for the balance your VPSA expects you to maintain between leading your portfolio and managing strategic institutional efforts. Take the time to question how the portfolio came to be and how it has changed over time. As you learn your new role, it might become clear that your supervisor wants the majority of your focus to be on developing the talent of your staff, deepening student engagement, and creating a culture of robust assessment within your portfolio. In these circumstances, it may make sense to have a relatively flat portfolio, where all of the units in your oversight area report directly to you. Although this is time consuming, it puts you in close contact with your directors and allows you to lead with the nuance your VPSA desires. However, if your supervisor wants you to focus the majority of your energy on the institutional strategic plan or on regional and national fundraising efforts, then you might want to consider a layered portfolio structure that reduces the number of direct reports you have to manage. In the latter scenario, creating pods or teams that report to a team leader, an executive director, or an assistant dean allows you to supervise a few people, rather than 8 to 10 directors. The time you get back from this restructuring can be applied to the external initiatives your VPSA wants you to focus on.

Redefining Professional Development as an AVP

Your sense of what kind of professional development you need may evolve as you learn about the culture, staff members, opportunities, and challenges. When creating a professional development plan as an AVP, consider the following areas.

Self-directed learning. By the stage in your career when you are considering an AVP role, you should be aware of your professional gaps. Perhaps you have always struggled with mastering Microsoft Excel documents or you want to develop public speaking skills. Start with two questions: (a) What have you repeatedly gotten critical feedback on throughout your career? and (b) What technical gaps continue to hinder your ability to be more efficient at work? The answers can lay the foundation for how to approach professional development in your new role. Within the first year, you can also ask your supervisor, staff, or peers (directly or through a 360-degree evaluation process) on suggested areas of continuous improvement. Select the areas that if improved could significantly enhance your work and divisional goals.

Campus resources. Discover what institution-based professional development opportunities exist to augment your learning and development. Many colleges and universities have ongoing professional development sessions on topics such as creating more dynamic presentations, learning advanced functions of the Microsoft Office suite, using social media, designing websites, and many more.

Regional and national opportunities. As a senior leader, you are a brand ambassador for the division and the university who has the potential to attract attention to or from your campus depending on how and what you present and your levels of engagement in activities and with other professionals. Consider professional development opportunities for skill-based training at regional and national conferences, consortiums, and institutes to meet other people in similar roles and to share resources. Presenting and publishing (solo or with others) is another great way to share expertise on a particular topic and potentially collaborate with other leaders across the country.

Academic pursuits. Many AVP roles require a terminal degree, but the learning can continue. Courses on budgeting and finance, information technology, and human resources are just few areas that offer continued development. Foreign language competency is also valuable. There is no checklist for professional development in this role. Instead, take a critical look at your current professional gaps, take inventory of the resources available to you on campus and nationally, and create a plan to incorporate this learning into your first year and beyond.

Wisdom from Vice Presidents for Student Affairs

Much of the success of new AVPs is determined by their supervisors. To solicit advice from current supervisors, we conducted a brief, anonymous, online survey of sitting VPSAs. We received responses from 18 VPSAs across the United States. Given the focus of this chapter, we chose responses that focused on balancing the day-to-day and strategic responsibilities and responses that offered general advice for AVPs.

Finding a sustainable equilibrium between daily tasks and long-term strategic initiatives is a key challenge for all large leadership roles. One VPSA shared that she expects her AVP to maintain focus on long-range goals, while directing reports and managers to accomplish short-range needs and goals. This positions the AVP not as the person achieving the divisional goals, but as the leader who helps the department steer toward tangible outcomes.

Another respondent wanted his AVP to offset his professional weaknesses. Because AVPs face endless demands on their time and energy, choosing specific areas of focus is wise. A few respondents remarked that successful AVPs develop their staff members' ability to manage the day-to-day, which can liberate the AVP to engage in strategic projects. As noted earlier, it is critical for new AVPs to scan their portfolios to assess the strengths and weaknesses of their staff members. By investing in your teams, you can actually invest in your own successes, as their increased capacity propels your leadership.

To manage the first year successfully, one leader suggested blocking an hour a week to turn off e-mail and reflect on such questions as, "What have I learned this week?" and "What relationships do I need to take care of next week, based on what I learned this week?" This emphasis on reflection was echoed across a number of responses and serves as a powerful reminder to treat yourself not simply as a leader, but as a learner. Another respondent remarked that hiding in the office might allow new AVPs to get much work done, but strong relationships and a full integration into the campus community serve them better in the long run.

Successful directors most often work through relationships to accomplish departmental goals. This strategy carries over to being a successful new AVP, and building strong relationships with key faculty, student leaders, and community partners helps you have an impactful first year on the job.

Finally, several VPSAs noted that they wanted their AVPs to "share potentially hot issues with me" or "tell me what others are not telling me." As a new AVP, when you have coffee and lunch with dozens of stakeholders, you might hear information that your VPSA needs to know. Do not be afraid to share the good, the bad, and the ugly with your supervisor, because they need the full picture to succeed in their role as well.

Conclusion

Each AVP role looks different based on the type of institution, the portfolio of the position, and the challenges and opportunities within the division. In conclusion, there are three points to remember.

Learn the landscape. Understanding your supervisor's agenda, the budgetary realities of the institution, the goals of the division, and the performance of your direct reports provides a strong starting point for getting a lay of the land. Knowing these areas helps you gain context and identify where you need to exert the most time and effort during the first year.

Manage your day, or it will manage you. By using your administrative assistant, blocking off time to fulfill administrative duties, and learning to balance strategic initiatives with the day-to-day operations of the job, you can create a plan that maximizes your time in the office. Set clear priorities for your calendar and create systems that work for you to manage multiple projects. Know how and when you can say no gracefully to opportunities that do not advance the goals of the division.

Be both a generalist and a specialist. Though much of your work may be spent on larger strategic initiatives, you must also convey the specifics in the areas that report to you. Spend time learning more about the functional areas where you have less professional experience and make sure your staff bring you up to speed on the latest trends in their area, both at the university and national level. In one day, you might be asked about collegiate enrollment trends on the West Coast and how many meal plans are currently offered on campus. Commit time each week to learning more about the general functions of each area, especially as they relate to direct services to students.

In an effort to support your transition into the AVP role, and through your first 90 days, we have developed a checklist for you to keep handy and reference frequently. The AVP Checklist for Success (see Appendix A) lists some of the most helpful action items from the chapter, organized chronologically to help you execute them in the right order.

Reference

Watkins, M. (2003). *The first 90 days: Critical success strategies for new leaders at all levels.* Boston, MA: Harvard Business School.

Recommended Reading

Catmull, E. E., & Wallace, A. (2014). *Creativity, inc.: Overcoming the unseen forces that stand in the way of true inspiration.* New York, NY: Random House.

Frank, C. J., & Magnone, P. F. (2011). *Drinking from the fire hose: Making smarter decisions without drowning in information.* New York, NY: Portfolio.

Loehr, J., & Schwartz, T. (2005). *The power of full engagement: Managing energy, not time, is the key to high performance and personal renewal.* New York, NY: Free Press.

Schwartz, T., Gomes, J., & McCarthy, C. (2011). *The way we're working isn't working: The four forgotten needs that energize great performance.* New York, NY: Free Press.

Recommended Professional Development Events

ACUI Women's Leadership Institute
  http://www.acui.org/wli
  For women who aspire to or are in new leadership positions on campus.

NASPA Alice Manicur Symposium
  http://www.naspa.org/events/2014manicur
  Specifically designed for women considering a move to become a chief student affairs officer.

NASPA AVP Institute
  http://www.naspa.org/events/avp-institute
  An intensive program designed to support and develop AVPs in their unique roles on campus.

Single- Versus Multiple-AVP Structures

Jeanine A. Ward-Roof and Ashanti Hands

The typical way to explain the roles or structures of an organization is to focus on the organizational chart (Bolman & Deal, 2008). Student affairs professionals also describe their institutions or divisions by focusing on to whom their position reports or who reports to them. Winston and Creamer (1997) stated that the single most important resource found in higher education is the people who accomplish the work. Moreover, they suggested that staffing patterns and practices offer great insight into how the organization views the worth of their human resources. Therefore, examining the number of associate/assistant vice president (AVP) positions in an institution, the working relationships of the AVPs, to whom the positions report, and how these reporting lines have an impact on someone's work may offer more insight into the organizational structure of the institution than a review of the organizational chart.

Whether one or multiple AVPs report to the vice president for student affairs, the dynamics of each structure come with a myriad of rewards and challenges that are not often a part of the written narrative that guides a professional's work. Understanding the nuances of such reporting structures can empower and have a positive impact on AVPs' ability to successfully address their numerous roles, navigate reporting lines, manage relationships, and maximize success.

This chapter includes relevant literature on current and innovative student affairs AVP structures, feedback from current and past AVPs regarding their roles, and our own experiences and insights. We focus on single- versus multiple-AVP structures and address similarities, differences, innovative practices, and tips for AVPs to be successful, regardless of the structure in which they work.

Why Structures Matter

Structures provide direction internally and externally regarding hierarchy and how decisions are made; moreover, structures reveal the culture of a campus and the amount and kinds of resources needed to accomplish goals that align with division priorities. Winston Churchill once said, "We shape our buildings, and afterward our buildings shape us" (McLuhan & Zingrone, 1995, p. 62). Much like buildings, student affairs organizational structures are static constructs that once built continue to inform day-to-day activities. Knowledge of AVP structures and the impact they have on the work of AVPs can be instrumental in successfully navigating relationships and reporting lines.

Kuk (2009) stated that an evolution has shaped student affairs structures, defined roles, established reporting lines, and deciphered management and leadership needs. This evolution is a facet of how student affairs work is defined or redefined, and structures are how the work is organized within the institution. Moreover, Kuk described structures based on institution type; when compared with other types of institutions, the structures of colleges that offer only bachelor's degrees were described as having a smaller and more shallow organization, while those colleges and universities granting bachelor's and master's degrees encompassed more elaborate structures in order to address the more numerous student needs. Furthermore, those institutions labeled as research or doctoral-granting types were defined as more intricate due to their size and innate complexities. Finally, Kuk noted that community colleges that typically offer associate degrees have a complexity to their organizations that is very different from the other institution types. Specifically, she noted that student affairs and student service functions are often combined within community college structures and that reporting lines and titles may differ as well.

Regardless of the institution type, structures and organizations help outline roles for those involved in the educational process. When defining the AVP role on a campus, the type of institution has a great deal of influence in the position. Kuk's (2009) work illustrated that as the complexity of the institution increases, so does the need for more specialized roles. Indeed, based on our experiences, the complexity of the institution defines the AVP role and structure.

AVP Models: Single Versus Multiple

Little research is available regarding general organizational structures within student affairs (Kuk, 2009) as well as more specific AVP roles. Historical documents explain what a student affairs division should address and how staff should meet the developmental needs of students, but they offer little direction about how organizations should be structured (American Council on Education, 1949; Blimling & Whitt, 1998; Keeling, 2004; Miller, Bender, & Schuh, 2005; American Association for Higher Education, American College Personnel Association, & National Association of Student Personnel Administrators, 1998). While perspectives on structure are not provided, these documents do include excellent insights into best practices and can assist professionals with the development of structures that will support those practices. Most existing AVP structures on college campuses were conceived with the common expectation to meet student needs and focus on student learning. Within the AVP structures today, there are still a great deal of similarities and differences; however, the traditional model for AVP positions is either a single AVP or multiple AVPs within an organization. Variables that influence those structures are the supervisory responsibilities for functional areas or other staff members the positions encompass, whether the AVP or AVPs carry the title of assistant (or associate) vice president, and whether those who have the AVP responsibilities are assigned a different title. These variables as well as institution type and size, leadership style of vice presidents and presidents, and political environments can all influence an AVP role.

Similarities and Differences

Each type of AVP model offers value to the institution and division, helps realize the university and division mission, and at some level assists with the management and leadership in the student affairs organization. Among the similarities found in many of the identified AVP models are the requisites: These professionals must have a strong set of communication, supervision, and political negotiation skills; be able to work within a great deal of ambiguity; have high levels of emotional maturity; and are able to manage multiple tasks at one time. Many of these elements, as discussed in Chapter 1, are described as core competencies for AVPs. In addition, AVP structures divide workloads and roles and enable professionals in the divisions to gain clarity on reporting lines, political issues, and support for programs and services.

AVP roles typically have open access to the vice president. AVPs can help interpret what is occurring in the division or what concerns others have and clarify the vice president's thoughts and ideas to members of the division. Moreover, those in AVP roles typically represent the division or vice president in campuswide and community-based efforts, serve as the VPSA when needed, and traditionally serve as a conduit from the division to other aspects of the institution. The AVP role also places a professional at a higher level in an organization and therefore makes the AVPs more vulnerable during turbulent or transitional times. Therefore, articulating the value of an AVP role and supporting that value with data is more important than ever.

Ginsberg (2011) argued that historically the vision for higher education was developed by faculty; more recently this role has been usurped by those in the administration, a trend that Ginsberg pronounced dangerous. Administrators are perceived as not having the strong academic preparation that faculty do. Ginsberg added that the administration's lower priority on research and teaching and its focus on soft skills in the curriculum detract from a superior education. To establish a more collaborative vision, earlier work by Dungy (2003) suggests student affairs leadership should create strong connections with those across campus to enable others inside and outside the division to better understand the vital roles performed by staff as well as increase collaboration and lower the risk of becoming disassociated and devalued with those across campus.

Differences in AVP structures include the breadth and depth of roles, functional area reporting lines, and levels of involvement in the institutional governance. Professionals who work in a multiple-AVP structure often find their roles are more specific, such as being charged with coordinating human resources, managing the division's budget, or supervising a specific aspect of the division. One of the biggest differences found in any AVP structure concerns the people who serve in the roles and are at the center of the processes. Each person brings his or her own perceptions, style, and interpretations that influence how he or she serves in the AVP role. If the people change, what once was a successful or unsuccessful relationship between two AVPs, or between an AVP and vice president, can quickly turn.

Institutional size and complexity create other differences. Smaller institutions often have one AVP, or someone with a different title (e.g., dean, director) who has the same responsibilities as the traditional AVP; conversely, organizational models with numerous vice presidents and multiple campuses may include two or more AVPs with specific roles and responsibilities for multiple functional areas and staff members. History also plays a part in the AVP role, because the title that has traditionally been tied to certain responsibilities can be used to entice a more seasoned staff member who seeks advancement elsewhere to remain at the institution.

Political frameworks can also influence AVP roles; legislative mandates might affect the number of AVPs as well as how the AVP role is seen on campus. Past performance of the high-level AVP role may dictate current practices as well. For instance, if a past AVP performed poorly and drew a large salary, the AVP role may be perceived as useless or unmanageable; conversely, if past performance was stellar, the way might be clear for future growth and heightened levels of responsibility. The AVP role might also be influenced by leadership's perception that this staff member needs to be an alumni or someone who has been at the institution a long time to be successful. Depending on the individuals selected for these roles, this narrow perception leads either to stagnant leadership or a successful AVP who did not have to learn the institutional culture. Additionally, other divisional structures may dictate the AVP structure; for example, a VPSA would probably not want to oppose his or her colleagues regarding the number of AVPs employed. These types of issues may negatively affect the overall effectiveness of the division yet have no direct correlation with the current professional's tenure, making for a difficult situation to manage for an AVP.

Finally, the difference between the title of assistant versus associate vice president might also be influenced by politics. In many organizations, the difference between *assistant* and *associate* vice president may be negligible when the title is dictated by the culture of the organization and not by the duties associated with the position. At other institutions, the titles may be differentiated by status, access to campus resources (such as a designated parking place or athletic tickets), position level, or supervisory responsibilities. Many of these aspects are external to an AVP's role and influence but can greatly affect the professional serving in the AVP role.

Challenges and Successes

To supplement the limited literature that focuses on AVP reporting structures, we conducted an informal survey to explore single- and multiple-AVP structures. We highlight several challenges and successes identified by the survey respondents and address the issues in order to facilitate a greater understanding of the scope, challenge, and rewards of an AVP role.

Twenty-eight professionals responded from all types of institutions (note that not all respondents answered all questions): 22 served 0–5 years in the AVP role; six served 6 years or more. One person was a current VPSA, 13 were in an AVP role. There were six deans, one assistant or associate dean, and two directors. Six respondents worked at a research university, nine at a comprehensive college or university, five at a liberal arts college, and three at a community college or 2-year institution. Eight stated their institution served fewer than 10,000 students, seven were between 10,001 and 20,000, five were between 20,001 and 30,000, and three served more than 30,000 students. Nineteen worked at public institutions and four at private; one described the institution as rural, six as urban, four as residential, and seven as commuter. When asked to whom they report, one stated a president, two a provost, one a senior vice president, and 18 a vice president or provost.

Single-AVP Challenges

When asked about challenges innate to a single-AVP structure, comments from the respondents included the following:

No cohort of peers. An AVP who serves in a single-AVP structure can feel like they are alone and unable to brainstorm or find others with whom to confer. Although their role includes assisting the vice president and helping to lead and manage the division, managing all of their duties can be overwhelming and cause them to lose sight of the goals and vision of the division or have difficulty getting perspective on issues. We suggest that those who work in single-AVP roles find colleagues outside the division and institution with whom to network in order to stay relevant and have someone to share challenges and successes with as well as to solicit advice from. In addition, keeping the vision, mission, and goals of the division and institution in the forefront of decision making and conversations ensures you are always a part of the decision-making process.

Too much work. Often in single-AVP roles, the amount of work can be overwhelming for just two people. Trying to determine priorities and where others can assist with the workload is paramount to the success in a single-AVP structure. The vice president is typically focused on the big picture items and needs the AVP to help manage and lead some of the everyday tasks as well as the latest crises and innovative projects. This can confound the ability of the AVP to find a balance between work and home life that is important for sustainability and as a role model to other staff members. Although Chapter 8 more fully addresses issues of balance for AVPs, this chapter briefly touches on the topic and offers the following: Sharing the high-level work with seasoned directors might lessen the workload for the vice president and the AVP and help directors gain valuable skills to advance in their careers. If this strategy is chosen, setting priorities for the work is also important, because staff members can only do so much successfully during a finite period of time.

Too many hats. The increase of federal and state mandates, coupled with the increased complexity of student affairs work, continues to challenge staff. In single-AVP models, the AVP is often the person who has to implement the new mandates and determine how to ensure institutional compliance. Where possible, hiring someone or increasing the current staff's responsibilities can be effective; otherwise, AVPs have to consider how to manage these multiple tasks and prioritize what will be completed.

Division of duties. Student affairs staff members are always managing a new crisis, addressing a new trend, or leading a new issue. Determining what needs to be addressed and by whom can be a difficult task, especially if it means changing reporting structures. Finding time to have in-depth discussions with the vice president about these decisions can be equally challenging. Some AVP positions are always moving from one role to the next, and the academic year can bring unending crises that need to be managed. At some point, those in leadership have to discuss how to divide the duties, but until that occurs, quick decisions on small parts of the duties may be the only way to manage. For an AVP, being nimble and flexible are essential aspects of the role. Knowing when you can make decisions and when you have to wait for the vice president to do so is imperative.

Balancing act. The AVP is the main person with whom the vice president strategizes, plans, and shares confidential information, but often the

AVP does not directly supervise the areas under discussion. The AVP often has to discuss issues without being able to share the whole picture, facilitate change by suggesting different ways of moving forward, or interpret issues and concerns on behalf of the vice president to those who do not report to him or her. Developing strong communication skills is vitally important to balancing these roles. An AVP must be a good listener and become comfortable with having enough authority and power to be responsible without being in control. To be successful, an AVP must carefully negotiate politics; remain loyal; and hone leadership, management, and relationship development skills. Additionally, maintaining clear lines of communication and well-defined expectations with the vice president can provide clarity within the ambiguity of single-AVP structures.

Not enough staff members. When operating in a single-AVP structure, some things just do not get done. The AVP has only so much time in the day and so many duties that can be managed and led. Attempting to be all things can lead to burn out or feeling less than successful. Being able to respond to multiple demands often boils down to setting priorities and managing time. When establishing priorities with the vice president, know which responsibilities, if any, can be further delegated and how projects align with divisional and institutional goals. Such knowledge can reduce, alleviate, or eliminate individual responsibilities. Time is a commodity often given away freely; rethinking your meeting and agenda schedule (in particular with direct reports) can free up time to meet AVP demands, focus on what is important, and identify tasks that just keep AVPs busy versus those that produce successful outcomes.

Confusing roles and hierarchy. Reporting directly to the vice president who supervises several department directors creates confusion regarding roles and hierarchy. One director might view his or her role as equal to the AVP; if the vice president does not delineate the difference, the organization can suffer. For an AVP, clear and frequent communication regarding roles, responsibilities, and reporting is critical. Take advantage of opportunities to creatively reinforce organizational hierarchies and methods for moving efforts forward. Work with the vice president to identify and assume high-level division- or campuswide responsibilities that differentiate the AVP role from directors who report straight to the vice president, roles such as serving on accreditation or executive search committees, responding to large-scale campus crises, and acting in the absence of the vice president.

Multiple-AVP Challenges

When asked about challenges innate to a multiple-AVP structure, comments from the respondents included the following:

Equity among departments. Departments managed and led by AVPs can vary by size and complexity within a student affairs division. When there are multiple AVPs within a structure, such differences can create the perception (or sometimes reality) that the balance of work is not equitably distributed. Navigating such perceptions requires a great deal of acumen and knowledge of programs, services, and outcomes within the division. Ideally, student affairs structures are situated around divisional and institutional strategic plans and missions. In such instances, what is equitable may not always result in an equal distribution of work. However, a reorganization to correct such imbalances is often thwarted by factors such as budget, politics, timing, and historical context. In these instances, acknowledging structural limitations while paying close attention to relationships and the big picture may provide the strength needed to progress and see the value that each area brings to the whole.

AVPs as directors. In multiple-AVP structures, the AVPs not only provides administrative oversight for a cluster of student affairs departments, but they also may serve as deans or directors of their own unit. The difference between the two positions can be one of leading the vision versus serving others, leading a team versus being a part of it, or advocating for a specific program versus advocating on behalf of the division and institution. Shifting between the 30,000-foot view and operating in the weeds can indeed be challenging. Managing competing priorities is a challenge that is likely to persist within these structures. Although balancing competing priorities can be difficult, it is not impossible. Clarifying roles and responsibilities, establishing priorities, communicating effectively, managing your time, delegating tasks (when appropriate), and persevering are techniques for addressing the issues.

Hyper focus on areas. In multiple-AVP structures, administrators can become consumed by work in their functional areas. The desire to protect, preserve, and advocate for functions that fall within an AVP's portfolio has its place; however, it becomes a challenge when areas no longer collaborate or see their connection to the larger whole. The reasons for retreating into silos can range from the allocation of scarce resources (such as time, space, or money), a lack of leadership, and breakdown in communication, to losing sight of the big picture. Multiple-AVP structures can break down these silos by contributing to a culture of trust and interconnectedness; identifying and removing barriers that prevent opportunities to collaborate; and constantly realigning mission, vision, and goals across departments, areas, divisions and institutional levels.

Single-AVP Successes

When asked about success unique to a single-AVP structure, comments from the respondents included the following:

Getting things done quickly. Single-AVP structures have a built-in ability to be nimble. These structures are often preferred by AVPs because they provide a level of autonomy and a mechanism for making and implementing change more rapidly than in many multiple-AVP systems. Flat organization structures tend to have less bureaucracy and a broader span of control in areas of communication, decision making, and outcomes. Single-AVP structures often work best in smaller organizations.

Independent thinking and collaboration. Single-AVP structures require staff and managers to work closely together in ways that celebrate independent thinking and teamwork. Flat structures create the space for managers and staff to see their work in smaller parts and as a part of a whole. There is often less territorialism; less likelihood of duplicated efforts; and more freedom to creatively problem solve, cross-train, and work toward desired outcomes.

Costs. It costs less to run single-AVP structures. The savings can contribute to the overall success of a division by allocating those funds for the institution or by allowing resources to be distributed throughout the division in support of divisional and institutional goals.

Multiple-AVP Successes

When asked about success unique to a multiple-AVP structure, comments from the respondents included the following:

Peer relationships. The survey respondents resoundingly cited collegial relationships with peers as critical to the success of multiple-AVP structures, specifically the ability to positively partner with colleagues, opportunities for collaboration, and shared experiences with others who understand the responsibilities of the AVP position. Establishing meaningful relationships is often key to successfully navigating structures.

Human resources. In multiple-AVP structures, AVPs can stretch and flex strengths and talents in ways that ensure students receive the best experience. Such structures allow for resources to be leveraged vertically and horizontally and support to be provided when another AVP is inaccessible. Multiple-AVP structures are sometimes easier to manage, because of clear lines of communication, centralized decision making, clearly defined responsibilities, and a larger scope of responsibility within specific areas.

Of course, featured items are often predicated on good communication and synergy.

Best Practices

When it comes to understanding single- and multiple-AVP structures within a division of student affairs, one size does not fit all. One structure is not better than the other, and both come with benefits, challenges, rewards, and successes that can be leveraged to create opportunities that can have a positive impact on the work of AVPs. In addition to the challenges and rewards of single- and multiple-AVP structures, the following list of best practices was gleaned from our informal survey of current and previous AVPs and their personal experiences. We were partial to this feedback, because it provided practical tips that can be translated to best practices and assist AVPs in managing and leading their organizational structure. The following suggestions include both personal and professional best practices.

Build relationships and trust. Taking time to get to know others helps you adjust to campus culture and be accepted by others, and building trust establishes you as someone who is ethical and honest. Remember that you are only as good as your word.

Secure mentors. Mentors can help an AVP reason through tough situations, gain perspective, plan a career, and gain alternative insights. Mentors are fully invested in your success and can provide feedback in ways that may be more effective than feedback from a supervisor.

Establish a network of peers at other institutions. Along with mentors, finding others who can provide perspective can be helpful. Connecting with other AVPs through professional networks helps you create trusted systems through which you can benchmark, network, and strategize.

Collaborate. Collaboration is a hallmark of a great AVP. Learning this skill and continually practicing it show that you are willing to work together to make the campus or community better and to advance the goals of the institution. Working together broadens and deepens opportunities enabling everyone to respond to the issues being addressed. Although AVPs and other professionals have admirable skills sets and are able to accomplish a great deal on their own, joining with others to brainstorm can only create a more comprehensive response, program, or service.

Have regular meetings. Keeping the mission, vision, and goals in the forefront of your work enables you, as an AVP, to focus on what is most important in the division. Meeting to share ideas keeps the mission in the forefront of everyone's minds.

Develop your staff. Part of an AVP role is career development; other staff members might seek career advice from you (as one of the senior administrators in the division) as they determine their future plans. Empowering others in the organization to gain skills and experiences not only enables that division to accomplish more but allows professionals to strengthen skills sets and prepare for future roles.

Listen. Listening to concerns, issues, and messages is paramount to an AVP's success. Professionals often rush to find solutions when all the other person really wants is someone to listen. Discerning when you should listen without acting is a best practice that only grows stronger with use.

Don't avoid difficult conversations. Difficult situations are just that—difficult; however, the longer they are left unaddressed, the harder they can be to manage. Craft strategic messages that confront and de-escalate difficult situations so those involved can move forward and focus on the more important aspects of the division.

Compromise. A passion for education is what led many AVPs to the position. This passion can fuel competition and territorialism because of the personal efforts staff make when creating programs and responding to issues. Putting this competition and territorialism aside and focusing instead on what is best for the division or student success enhance the institution and ultimately strengthen the response the institution provides.

Be transparent. Developing a transparent and easily understood style will be well received by your coworkers. Typically, you have the luxury of time to address issues and create plans; including others in the process and having others take responsibility for certain aspects of a plan, a change, or a decision demonstrates transparency and inclusion.

Be an expert in your area. As AVP, you can be so busy with daily roles, you might forget to share knowledge or expertise. Share background on students, functional areas, trends, campus culture, and community perspectives with others in order to establish your expertise and assist others with decision making and future plans.

Maintain clear and constant communication. Communication is one of the most important aspects of any professional role. Clear and consistent communication with the vice president, AVPs, and direct reports enables everyone to understand goals, priorities, and current issues and can also establish division priorities and increase trust and collaboration between staff.

Keep the vice president in the loop. No vice president or any supervisor wants to be surprised. Developing a system to share important information is vitally important to the relationship between the AVP and the vice president. Moreover, using technology, meetings, and other venues to share information as needed enables an AVP to keep others informed in a timely and consistent manner.

Get clarity on positions and reporting lines. Role clarity leads to more effective execution and less ambiguity. Although every role cannot be completely defined, you can gain insight on bigger aspects of your position during the onboarding process or early on in your position. Ask questions to best understand both unwritten and written expectations.

Understand campus culture. Transitioning to a new campus or role requires time and diligence on the part of the staff members and the institution. Formal programs, such as orientation, offer insights into campus culture. Learn how the processes work and where the informal and formal power exists. As an AVP, learning about campus culture on a new campus or from a new level in the organization can help you remove barriers or misunderstandings in the future.

Innovative Directions

Although AVPs have a choice in how they respond to an issue or perform in a structure, AVPs do not always have a say in the organizational structure of a division. When those opportunities do arise or you are asked to rethink leadership and management issues in the organizational structure, knowing the current literature, trends, and campus culture can help you offer insightful and relevant information. When discussing innovative directions for organizational structures within student affairs, look to the literature on the subject for a range of strategies.

Bolman and Deal (2008) offered a unique perspective for determining how to best design and lead today's complex organizations. They suggested that four frames be considered: symbolic, political, structural, and human resource. Though each provides critical pieces of information that can lead to substantive change within an organization, we focus here on the structural and human resource frames; they provide great context for innovative directions when reconsidering AVP structures and managing aspects of a divisional structure. Bolman and Deal's structural frame centers on the allocation of responsibilities and establishing connections across divisional areas while pursuing common goals. Both single- and multiple-AVP structures benefit from purposeful rethinking and reorganization by keeping concepts such as rules, roles, goals, and policies in mind.

Bolman and Deal's (2008) human resource frame centers on relationships, skills, and needs of the people in an organization. AVPs involved in innovating student affairs structures benefit from creating synergy between the organization and its people. Doing so provides a mechanism for meeting the needs of staff, while the staff in turn successfully meet the needs of the organization. Access to professional development and networking is paramount to an AVP and those whom the AVP supervises. Exploring and institutionalizing innovative and unique professional development options for yourself and for those you supervise can be rewarding and can develop a stronger staff. In considering innovative directions in multiple- and single-AVP structures, the human resource frame allows administrators to be mindful of creating the right conditions for professional and student success.

In researching organizational structures in student affairs, Kuk and Banning (2009) found that innovative directions have roots in aligning student affairs structures with institutional mission, strategic goals, and objectives—not just historical, cultural, or personality-based context. The researchers also implied that innovative student affairs structures should be designed to strategically address new challenges and foster collaborations within and across units and divisions. Institutionalizing systems that align missions and foster collaboration position AVPs to effectively and efficiently respond to challenges and adapt to changes on issues ranging from diversity, equity, and inclusion, to service delivery and the enforcement of local, state, and federal mandates.

When you are defining an AVP structure or redefining certain aspects of a division's organization, we suggest you benchmark with similar institutions for insights into the numerous types of AVP roles and organizational structures possible. This provides you several options for building the best model on your campus. Keep in mind that innovation from anywhere in the organization can be helpful. When serving in an AVP role, take time to understand and listen to the students, the faculty, the staff, the division, and the institution to better serve those with whom you work.

Conclusion

Serving as an AVP is both challenging and rewarding; the role requires someone to lead aspects of a division without leading the entire division, to spend time at the 30,000-foot level and in the weeds, to help professionals meet their goals, and to determine what is important personally. The AVP role also requires responsiveness, innovativeness, and timeliness as well as the ability to interpret for and to the vice president. Serving as an AVP is a huge responsibility and one that is vital to the success of many student affairs divisions. As we close this chapter, we offer the following key points to ponder:

Structure. Understanding and negotiating the organizational structure is an important aspect of an AVP role.

- Bolman and Deal (2008) provided insights on the value of focusing on the whole organization despite supervising only smaller facets of an organization. Consider especially the structural and human resources frames for successful decision making.
- Winston and Creamer (1997) identified human resources as the greatest resource in student affairs. Helping to create policy and practices that keep human resources at the forefront of decision making—while considering the frames discussed by Bolman and Deal (2008)—can positively influence the success of an AVP and an entire student affairs division.
- Structures can be cumbersome, but they help others understand processes, leadership, and goals. They also identify priorities and shape behaviors; an AVP's understanding of structures within an institution can open doors and determine who might be successful partners.

- Institution type can greatly influence structure and all resources. We applied Kuk's (2009) insights to traditional AVP models, offering another perspective for student affairs professionals to consider when designing AVP structures or determining how to find fit as an AVP.
- The outcomes described in historical student affairs documents can be used to design AVP structures and AVP supervisory models and to meet student needs.
- The two traditional types of AVP structures—multiple- or single-AVP staffing models—have many similarities and differences.

The AVP role. Negotiating the nuances, levels, and politics of an AVP role is challenging and requires strategic thinking; at the same time, other aspects of the role are controlled externally.

- Many variables influence the AVP position: functional area and staff reporting lines; position title, whether assistant or associate vice president, or having no AVP title (but similar responsibilities); institution type and size; the leadership styles of your supervisor and the president; and the political environment.
- AVP positions should offer value to the division and institution in which they report, should help to realize the mission, and should lead the organization in some manner. Identifying the value of your role as AVP and articulating it to others is part of a successful execution.
- Common traits for AVP professionals are strong communication, supervision, and political skills; the ability to work in a great deal of ambiguity; a high level of emotional maturity; and the ability to successfully multitask.
- Typically, AVPs have open access to the vice president and can help clarify messages from or to that person; in addition,

- traditionally, AVPs have broad roles that take them throughout the university and into the community, especially when the vice president is unable to do so.
- Professionals in AVP roles are more vulnerable during turbulent and transitional times. Collaborative connections across campus can lessen the vulnerability and lower the risk of being devalued (Dungy, 2003).
- Political frameworks also shape the AVP position on a campus; whether legislative mandates, alumni pressure, or the past performance of an AVP, all can positively or negatively affect the success of the incumbent AVP. Often the AVP has little ability to change these frameworks, but awareness helps the AVP negotiate the campus successfully.
- There is no one best AVP structure; the best structure is what works for the institution. Moreover, innovative practices—such as aligning student affairs structures with institutional mission, strategic goals, and objectives; creating conditions that matter; and benchmarking—help AVPs fulfill their roles.

References

American Association for Higher Education, American College Personnel Association, & National Association of Student Personnel Administrators. (1998). *Powerful partnerships: A shared responsibility for learning: A joint report*. Retrieved from http://www.myacpa.org/sites/default/files/taskforce_powerful_partnerships_a_shared_responsibility_for_learning.pdf

American Council on Education. (1949). *The student personnel point of view*. Retrieved from http://www.myacpa.org/student-personnel-point-view-1949

Blimling, G. S., & Whitt, E. J. (1998). Principles of good practice for student affairs. *About Campus, 3*(1), 10.

Bolman, L., & Deal, T. (2008). *Reframing organizations: Artistry, choice and leadership* (4th ed.). San Francisco, CA: Jossey-Bass.

Dungy, G. J. (2003). Organization and functions of student affairs. In S. R. Komives & D. B. Woodward, Jr. (Eds.), *Student services: A handbook for the profession* (4th ed., pp. 339–357). San Francisco, CA: Jossey-Bass.

Ginsberg, B. (2011). *The fall of the faculty: The rise of the all-administrative university and why it matters*. New York, NY: Oxford University Press.

Keeling, R. (Ed.). (2004). *Learning reconsidered: A campus-wide focus on the student experience*. Washington, DC: American College Personnel Association and National Association of Student Personnel Administrators.

Kuk, L. (2009). The dynamics of organizational models within student affairs. In G. S. McClellan & J. Stringer (Eds.), *The handbook of student affairs administration* (3rd ed., pp. 313–332). San Francisco, CA: Jossey-Bass.

Kuk, L., & Banning, J. H. (2009). Designing student affairs organizational structures: Perceptions of senior student affairs officers. *NASPA Journal, 46*(1), 94–117.

McLuhan, E., & Zingrone, F. (Eds.). (1995). *Essential McLuhan.* New York, NY: Basic Books.

Miller, T. E., Bender, B. E., & Schuh, J. H. (2005). *Promoting reasonable expectations: Aligning student and institutional views of the college experience.* San Francisco, CA: Jossey-Bass.

Winston, R., & Creamer, D. (1997). *Improving staffing practices in student affairs.* San Francisco, CA: Jossey-Bass.

Leadership and Strategic Planning
A Blend of the Visionary and Practical

Nancy Crimmin and Pauline Dobrowski

How are leadership and strategic planning defined for the associate/assistant vice president (AVP) of student affairs? This simple question, which pairs two complex functions, goes beyond traditional graduate-coursework definitions and case studies to the practical and rapidly changing realities of 21st-century campuses. The AVP is called to navigate increasingly complex legal issues, fast-moving technologies, and ever-changing campus environments, while addressing and managing diverse needs, hopes, and dreams of the student population (Scheuermann, 2011).

Leadership for the AVP generally requires managing one or

more functional areas while maintaining a pivotal role on the vice president for student affairs' (VPSA) management team. One of the most critical areas an AVP generally contributes to and assists the VPSA with is strategic planning. Specific roles and responsibilities for the AVP within strategic planning vary as much as their roles vary across campuses. This chapter provides context for balancing the day-to-day oversight of multiple functional areas while simultaneously contributing to divisional and institutional leadership in a role that is distinctly in the middle. In addition, situational vignettes throughout the chapter provide opportunities to pause and reflect on real-life scenarios that AVPs often encounter.

Leadership Defined

Northhouse (2007) defined leadership as "a process whereby an individual influences a group of individuals to achieve a common goal" (p. 3). Although the research identified a multitude of theoretical approaches to best define this concept, it is clear that leadership is a core competency that involves process, influence, and goal attainment generally within the context of a larger group (Northhouse, 2007). Leadership is also contingent on developing and managing core relationships.

Administrative leadership on college and university campuses is difficult to define because of the complex nature of a hierarchy that has varying patterns of structure and delegation. The structure of administrative governance fluctuates according to institutional size, mission, sponsorship, tradition, and values (Birnbaum, 1988). No better example of this complexity exists than the staffing practices and patterns within student affairs divisions. Defined by Winston and Creamer (1997) as "the institutional-level organizational unit responsible for dealing with the out-of-class lives of students," student affairs divisions range from multilayered structures with functional area specialists to teams of "professional generalists—staff who carry out multiple roles in service to students" (p. 4).

Leadership structures within student affairs are not always consistent, making the process of defining individual positions challenging to both generalize and operationally define (Bennett & Miles, 2006; Birnbaum, 1988; Winston & Creamer, 1997). Often, the organizational structure is hierarchical: The VPSA oversees one or more AVPs, who in turn oversee smaller units within the division led by directors, coordinators, assistants, or associates. This hierarchical structure results "in an administratively domineering character for most divisions of student affairs where certain staff—those charged with managerial responsibility—act as leaders for other staff" (Winston & Creamer, 1997, p. 5). As discussed in the previous chapter, some divisions have multiple-AVP positions, while others have one, and position titles can vary widely (e.g., dean of students, executive director, senior director).

How can a title accommodate such diversity and still be meaningful? Although many leadership positions are primarily defined by the work to be done (e.g., the director of residence life manages the housing system on campus), the AVP role is defined in relation to the VPSA's vision and the AVP's ability to effectively navigate relationships—both within the division as well as within the larger institutional environment. Regardless of the title or organizational structure, successful leadership, particularly in relation to strategic planning, depends on the AVP's ability to understand, interpret, and support the VPSA's vision across multiple levels throughout the institution.

Leading Distinctly From the Middle

Although AVPs traditionally do not categorize themselves as middle managers, the typical hierarchical structure of student affairs divisions places this position distinctly in the middle. AVPs serve as a bridge between senior leadership, whose focus is the overall strategic vision for the institution, and those overseeing the functional units within the division, thus requiring the AVP to successfully translate strategy into results both within and outside the division.

Research and literature on the AVP position in student affairs is meager, but the corporate world offers information on how to succeed within this position. Hytner (2014) created a model for leadership based on the *consiglieri*—the advisors to leaders of Italian mafia families—made famous by Mario Puzo's 1969 novel *The Godfather*. The *consiglieri* in Hytner's work are the advisors, the deputies, and the counselors—all who support, inform, and advise the final decision makers in an organization. Much like the *consiglieri*, leaders in student affairs at the AVP level should imbibe a strong sense of professional and personal purpose and demonstrate a commitment to the organization as well as loyalty to their supervisor(s). Although the bosses (i.e., the VPSAs) are most closely associated with leading the vision, the *consiglieri* (i.e., the AVPs) actively infuse that vision with credibility through their work, which often extends beyond the traditional boundaries of their spheres of influence within the larger organization. Without the AVP who has the skills to serve as the conduit between senior leadership and those managing the day-to-day operations, it would be difficult to translate the articulated vision into action.

Other research on middle management in the corporate world can be applied to the unique and critical leadership responsibilities of the AVP within student affairs. Specifically, in a 6-year study of 200 midlevel managers, Huy (2001) found that they were valuable contributors to the success of the organization, because they were distinctly positioned to implement change and communicate effectively across all levels of the organization. Huy's research suggested that those in the middle add value because they understand the core values of the organization, which helps them lead, manage, and implement the overall corporate strategy.

Whether this unique middle manager is helping lead a major corporation or a student affairs division, the AVP must hold a particular set of competencies. Heffernan (2011) stated, "New leadership of higher education is seeking leaders with a complex set of characteristics and experiences" (p. 117). In order to be influential, the AVP's skill set should include expertise and relevant experience. Demonstrating exceptional leadership both within the division and across the institution is a fundamental competency that requires ongoing development and reflection.

Leadership as a Critical Competency

In 2015, a joint task force composed of members from both the American College Personnel Association (ACPA) and National Association of Student Personnel Administrators (NASPA) developed and published a document that described a set of professional competency areas that "lay out essential knowledge, skills, and dispositions expected of all student affairs educators, regardless of functional area or specialization within the field" (p. 7). Each competency area includes a specific skill set needed for basic, intermediate, and advanced levels of proficiency. These competencies are critical to master, because AVPs may be called on at any time to assume the role of the VPSAs in their absence, as well as take on additional senior responsibilities as necessary.

Leadership, one of the 10 identified competencies, "involves both the individual role of a leader and the leadership process of individuals working together to envision, plan, and affect change in organizations and respond to broad-based constituencies and issues" (ACPA & NASPA, 2015, p. 27). Given the requirements and expectations of the AVP role, this competency necessitates the acquisition and development of certain skills noted within the advanced outcomes, specifically related to the development, promotion, and implementation of a shared vision. A recent scan of online job postings for traditional AVP positions revealed the desire for collaborative, creative, and committed leaders who support student success and can assist the VPSA to shape the vision and drive both short- and long-term planning. This reflects the need for advanced skills and competencies.

"Vision is a central component of great leadership" (Atkins, 2010, p. 23). Atkins (2010) wrote that leaders must align their vision to the overall institution's mission and that "a good vision clarifies the general direction for change, motivates people to take action in that right direction, and helps coordinate the action of different people in a fast and efficient manner" (p. 23). By collaborating and communicating within and outside the division and establishing productive relationships with their counterparts in other programmatic divisions, AVPs can offer a holistic and blended perspective for developing a shared vision. Student affairs leaders who are able to develop, articulate, and garner support for a well-defined vision, both at a divisional and institutional level, can establish a strong foundation for creating and executing an effective strategic plan.

Strategic Planning

Welsh, Nunez, and Petrosko (2005) wrote, "Strategic planning is one of the most persuasive and, arguably, most important management activities in higher education at the beginning of the 21st century" (p. 20). Higher education, similar to other industries, is searching for innovative ways to respond within a time of rapid change. As Keeling (2004) stated,

> A remarkable number of social and cultural trends, economic forces, population changes, new and emerging technologies, and issues of public policy will have powerful and lasting effects on the ability of colleges and universities to fulfill the demands of their mission and the expectations of their students and constituencies. (p. 6)

Leadership and Strategic Planning

Therefore, in order to survive and prosper within this type of environment, institutional leaders must be visionary in their approach and strategic in their thinking.

Kotler and Murphy (1981) defined strategic planning as "the process of developing and maintaining a strategic fit between the organization and its changing marketing opportunities" (p. 471). It is a process through which leaders can bring visibility to issues facing the institution and inspire people toward a common vision (Ellis, 2010). As Kloppenberg (2004) stated, "Today, strategic planning is most effective if it sets the stage for a continued process through which key constituents examine 'who we are' as an institution, 'where we are going,' and 'what we need to do' to get there" (p. 103). Due to the critical nature of this type of work and the potential future ramifications to the viability and success of institutions, visionary and effective leadership is needed within this area.

What is the AVP's leadership role within strategic planning? Using the findings from a survey of chief student affairs officers by NASPA's Research and Policy Institute, Wesaw and Sponsler (2014) sought to identify, among many things, how VPSAs manage the complex daily operations of their divisions. Data revealed that VPSAs ranked strategic planning within the top three administrative issues on their campuses. VPSAs also indicated that although their ideal allocation of time spent on strategic planning was 18%, their actual allocation of time spent was only 12%. Given that VPSAs spend only two thirds of their desired time to this critical administrative issue, it is not surprising that much of the responsibility within this area falls to the AVP within the division.

Strategic planning requires a constant blend of both institutional and functional perspectives. The AVP is well positioned to strike a balance between the visionary and the practical. The AVP must be an innovative leader and strategic thinker, without losing sight of the daily work within the division. Mills (2009) noted that "the middle manager acts as

> **Creating a Shared Vision**
>
> *You are sitting with your VPSA as she is outlining her vision for the division moving forward. As she shares her thinking and some of the strategic initiatives tied to her vision, you cannot help but consider how this will be received by your directors. How will you communicate this plan to your directors in a way that creates a shared vision? How will these initiatives affect the current operations within the individual departments? How will financial and personnel resources need to shift or be reallocated to meet this vision? As your mind starts to wander, you catch yourself and focus your attention back on her and her vision.*

a strategy ambassador bringing information about institutional strategy to front-line workers and bringing front-line knowledge back to executives. The cascade of information in this paradigm flows both downward and upward" (p. 360). This approach illustrates the hallmark of the distinctly unique middle-management role of the AVP. The critical exchange of information promotes communication and transparency within the leadership hierarchy, allows for issues to be identified and addressed in a timely manner, and intentionally engages stakeholders in developing a shared plan.

AVPs effectively translate their VPSAs' vision to their direct reports in order to generate buy-in and support for the strategic plan by:

- ensuring a clear and comprehensive understanding of the VPSA's vision and asking clarifying questions, including how and why the vision contributes to institutional success;
- articulating the vision to direct reports in a manner that communicates purpose and value and inspires them to visualize their units' contributions;
- encouraging ongoing reflection on how to operationalize the vision within their daily work;

Leadership and Strategic Planning

- facilitating dialogue and solicit constructive feedback that can be shared with the VPSA; and
- ensuring that those primarily affected by the vision feel supported and have the resources necessary to implement the plan.

Admittedly, developing a shared vision for a strategic plan can be complicated work. To keep people motivated and focused on achieving the stated goals, the AVP needs to emphasize the desired outcomes and how they subsequently translate into institutional effectiveness and student success. Trust and credibility in the process, as well as the ability to successfully collaborate across individual areas and the institution as a whole, are imperative. Established and productive working relationships are at the heart of this process.

Managing Relationships and Building Partnerships

Effective leadership, within strategic planning and other management functions, is contingent upon the AVP's capability to develop and

> **Cultivating Positive Working Relationships**
>
> *You are the only AVP under the VPSA in a student affairs division at a small college. You are proud of the relationship you've built with your VPSA. Based on trust and common goals, the two of you seem to click on every level. Concurrently, you have worked hard to do the same with your direct reports. Cultivating relationships, building trust, and taking the time to enjoy some humor along the way have helped develop solid working relationships with appropriate boundaries. You feel confident everyone is on the same page. How do you manage if this is not your reality? What strategies can you use to create more positive and effective working relationships?*

sustain effective working relationships. Roper (2002) contended that "our success as student affairs professionals is more closely tied to our ability to construct and manage essential relationships during our careers than to any other activity" (p. 11). Reisser and Roper (1999) concluded, "The common denominator for all levels of management is human relations skill—ability and judgment of working with and through people" (p. 126). AVPs are often challenged to define how they relate to and connect with their VPSAs and, in turn, how they forge relationships with those they supervise.

Managing the relationship and assessing the relative match between the AVP and the VPSA ultimately begins with the approach taken during the hiring process. Experienced and savvy VPSAs understand that their success, and the success of the division, is dependent on the talent of a leadership team. A VPSA may be looking for an AVP with a similar personality and work style in order to best ensure the relationship can be easily maintained. However, other VPSAs may approach the hiring process more strategically by seeking an AVP with qualities, characteristics, skills, and experiences that complement their work style. It is critical for AVPs to have a full understanding of how their VPSAs' work style and leadership match, oppose, or complement their own work style. Strategically choosing an AVP who is additive and not repetitive brings a different dynamic, because it creates a more holistic leadership team within the division. Should a VPSA assume the role where an AVP is already in place, the AVP must quickly assess work style in order to begin the process of building a partnership, while guiding the VPSA in assimilating into the new role.

The quality of the relationships AVPs have with others can have a powerful impact, both positively and negatively, on the ability to be productive and efficient in all leadership aspects. Because of the demanding and ever-changing dynamic of the academic workplace, taking time to build and sustain effective relationships is not always a high priority.

Neglecting this effort can lead to a lack of trust and loyalty (Bennett & Miles, 2006; Hytner, 2014; Roper, 2002; Scheuermann, 2011; Winston & Creamer, 1997).

Research in both business and higher education consistently identifies trust within a working relationship as crucial to success, which can clearly be seen within the relationship of AVPs and their VPSAs. Due to the power differential between an employee and a supervisor, those who are early in their career might tend to approach the relationship tentatively and in a deferential manner (Roper, 2002). "Such an approach deprives the supervisor of a needed colleague while also extinguishing a perspective that may be crucial to an organization's success" (Roper, 2002, p. 17). Levinson, Humphrey, Evans, and Berry (1993) described the relationship between a supervisor and their second as complex and a "balancing act on the threshold of power" (p. 71).

Individuals understand and demonstrate their power and authority in different ways. Thus, AVPs should recognize and manage the relationship with the VPSAs based on the power dynamic present within their relationship. The AVPs and VPSAs must be able to identify and articulate their approaches to power, because their approaches relate to their leadership roles.

French and Raven (1959) conducted a study analyzing power in leadership roles. Their study identified five bases of power and how each one can have an impact on a leader's ability to succeed within the designated role:

- **Legitimate:** having the position of authority to make demands and expect compliance from others.
- **Reward:** the ability to compensate others, in tangible and intangible ways, for doing what is wanted or expected of them.
- **Expert:** possessing the expertise, knowledge, and ability to be effective within the organization.

- **Referent:** using shared beliefs and connections within the group—combined with a level of admiration for the leader—to produce positive, correlated actions.
- **Coercive:** using the threat of force (social, emotional, or financial) to gain compliance from others.

Managing relationships and building partnerships within the context of power for the VPSA and AVP may be best achieved by a combination of expert and referent power. These two positions require a relationship based on mutual respect, trust, and credibility, which can ultimately inspire collective action and serve as a model of shared leadership within other levels of the division.

A VPSA once described relationships in terms of "practicing the principle of encouraging openness and honesty within our organization [so that] members will function as good colleagues to one another and to the senior student affairs officer" (Roper, 2002, p. 16). As in any trusting relationship between an AVP and a VPSA, there must be a mutual sense of investment. To assume the VPSA will always be kind in approach, transparent with communication, unselfish with praise, and pleasant to be around is unrealistic. The same is also true for the AVP. However, confidence in each other and a shared commitment must be at the center of this professional relationship. Loyalty conveys a strong sense of trust and demonstrates to supervisors that they can count on the employees to be there for them, especially in challenging times (Hytner, 2014; Roper, 2002). Roper (2002) reported personal reflections from a VPSA speaking to the issues of trust and loyalty:

> What I learned as a boss myself, but did not fully appreciate as a young professional, was that loyalty is the glue of friendship between leaders and followers. It does not mean one gives up independence and principled critique but that one tempers them with a good deal of practical judgment.

I learned as a boss that there are many times when what one wants and needs is a sounding board, a receptive and trusted person who will listen and not judge, unless requested to do so. Complete loyalty, of course, must ultimately be given only to those one can respect. But I believe loyalty is a virtue that one should practice with all bosses, at least to the point where it cannot be given in good conscience. Leadership can be a lonely business, and loyalty is one of the important ways in which bosses recognize trust and goodwill and build upon it in professional relationships. (p. 18)

In order for a positive relationship to exist, the VPSA must have confidence that the AVP is getting the job done. One of the most effective ways to establish a strong foundation is to develop clear and operationally defined goals, as well as a method for attainment and assessment. If VPSAs know the AVPs have comprehensive and integrated plans for their individual areas to meet their goals and objectives, and the plans are working, the temptation for the VPSAs to insert themselves into the process is drastically diminished.

To manage the relationship with the VPSA, consider the following strategies:

- Be an implementer and overseer, managing individual areas effectively and efficiently.
- Form strong lines of communication with the VPSA. How often does the VPSA want updates and in what form? Which decisions can the AVP have the final say on and which ones need VPSA input and approval? What issues would the VPSA like to know about immediately and which ones can wait? How do you approach difficult conversations?
- Create an environment of support and accountability so that each level of the organization manages its area in an effort to keep problems where they belong and at the level where they can best be addressed.

> **Maximizing Potential and Inspiring Engagement**
>
> *Your new position as an AVP at a midsize institution presents many new challenges for you as a leader. You now supervise four directors and most of them have been at the institution for many years. It quickly becomes clear that your new staff has valuable skills; however, many are not working to their full potential. What strategies do you use to develop positive working relationships with your direct reports? How do you identify the factors that influence and motivate your direct reports? What excites them about their work and how can you use information in their job performance plan? What skills do you use to personalize your supervision for each of your direct reports?*

- Learn to take the lead without overshadowing your VPSA. The VPSA should feel supported by the AVP; the AVP should not overstep into the VPSA role.

Many, if not all, of these strategies can also be applied to the relationship between the AVP and direct reports.

In order to effectively manage relationships with direct reports, the AVP needs to build trust and credibility both with individual managers and the team as a whole while maximizing transparency through ongoing and open communication. The leadership approach for the AVP must be customized for all direct reports based on their individual skill sets and experience, learning styles, and professional needs, including how they receive and respond to constructive feedback. By doing so, the AVP is best able to identify the skills and competencies of each direct report and how each can best contribute to the work of the division. Ultimately, the direct reports feel motivated to do their best work and feel like valued members of the team. The ultimate goal of managing these relationships and building partnerships is to establish a unified team within the division that can positively contribute to the overall mission of the institution.

Good leadership creates a structure in which individual relationships develop and staff understand what it means to be a team (Roper, 2002). The variance in administrative structures, organizational cultures, campus environments, and most important the personality and professional tendencies of the VPSA creates a need for an AVP who has a strong combination of practical, professional competence and relationship maturity (Bennett & Miles, 2006; Hytner, 2014, Roper, 2002; Walton, 2012). Relationship maturity, as defined by Roper (2002), is the ability to balance our need to assert an independent perspective with our loyalty to those with whom we are in a relationship.

True leaders also understand the need for allowing the talent of others to shine and providing the opportunity for multiple voices to be heard. Therefore, AVPs should promote the good work of their direct reports to a greater audience, including the VPSA. When AVPs build encouraging and caring relationships with their colleagues, they do not take credit for the successes of others but they can feel a sense of pride at being connected to that success. As former U.S. president Harry Truman said, "It's amazing what you can accomplish when you do not care who gets credit for it" (Harry S. Truman Biography, n.d.).

Managing Relationships Within the Strategic Planning Process

The concept of managing relationships and building partnerships is a critical component to successful strategic planning. Although the content of the final document is important, the process of creating a strategic plan is often more important. A process that allows for all voices to be heard and generates buy-in can facilitate the execution of the plan, which is largely left to the AVP and direct reports.

Kloppenberg (2004) described a process that "fosters an ongoing atmosphere where people can be creative, advance constructive criticism, and continually seek improvement" (p. 104). She continued that it must be "an inclusive process where people from multiple constituencies could speak honestly while striving to keep the process focused and moving ahead toward action" (p. 105). This type of atmosphere can exist only where trust exists and positive relationships have been established and continue to be nurtured, which could present an ongoing challenge for the AVP during the strategic planning process.

Oftentimes, the AVP is responsible for identifying and bringing colleagues together from multiple divisions to develop a strategic plan. The group must be expansive and include those who represent various facets of the institution. Acknowledging that in this setting individuals have their own perspectives and beliefs, the AVP needs to develop a shared sense of purpose among the group and facilitate relationship building in order to broaden everyone's thinking and maximize the effectiveness of the work. As Kloppenberg (2004) stated, "At its best, strategic planning can strengthen a sense of shared challenges, calling our colleagues to collaborative enterprise despite the highly individualized incentives within academic institutions" (p. 103). This spirit of collaboration is at its best when the AVP establishes a culture of respect and credibility within the group and encourages active listening, open dialogue, and consensus building (Conneely, 2010).

What happens when the spirit of collaboration breaks down? Managing human resources and navigating campus politics play a vital role in building strong teams able to assess and navigate complex processes, such as strategic planning. This does not imply that the AVP should assemble a team whose members are of similar mind and style. Quite the contrary, teams should be composed of those across divisions with varying, yet well-intended,

Leadership and Strategic Planning

approaches, perspectives, experiences, and agendas so that the AVP can best challenge the group to think critically and consider issues more broadly.

Within the strategic planning process, faculty is an important constituent group for the AVP to partner with and engage, because their contributions and commitment to a plan are essential to the plan's viability and implementation. Whitney (2010) contended that

> the answer to why faculty should work with student affairs professionals to create and implement a strategic plan involves maximizing talent and expertise, responding to increased competition for funding, increasing the reputation of the university in an increasing competitive market, and capitalizing on learning efficacy for students. (p. 64)

Involving faculty in conversations about the future direction within student affairs generates a deeper level of understanding and support for your work and strengthens relationships with its members.

Given the nature of the role, the AVP often has a pulse on what is going on in the day-to-day lives of students. To ensure that the student perspective is represented in the strategic planning process, the AVP can engage the student body in conversations about the future direction of the institution and what they want from the student experience. As with other stakeholders, student buy-in regarding a strategic plan is critical, because it can add significant credibility and generate enthusiasm for the plan.

Depending on the organizational size and structure, the AVP, even prior to the start of a strategic planning process, may be uniquely positioned to best understand, interpret, and leverage the student voice. Whether through attending student government meetings, interacting in the residence halls, or traveling on service immersion trips, AVPs can observe student life in a way that allows the student experience to continually inform their work. Understanding the student experience is most important when an institution's culture does not lend itself to leveraging and appreciating the student voice. In these instances, the AVP must get students involved in concrete

> **Centering On Our Students**
>
> *You just finished up your weekly divisional leadership meeting where you and your VPSA reviewed the most updated draft of the divisional strategic plan with the group. You are happy with the overall direction of the plan thus far, and the directors provided some insightful feedback on some of the specific initiatives. You head in the direction of the student union building where you will now be meeting with the Student Government Association to present the draft plan to them. In addition to ongoing conversations you've been having with university leadership and your direct reports about the plan, you have been very intentional about soliciting student feedback to ensure that the student voice is clearly represented within the document. However, you are keenly aware that much of their feedback is not reflected in the current draft. You enter the meeting and are greeted by a group of student leaders, eager to receive an update. How do you best approach this conversation to try to maintain their engagement within the process while representing the wider institutional perspective?*

ways: hold town hall meetings, get students on planning committees, talk with students at student government meetings, conduct focus groups, and get their feedback on drafts of the plan. The AVP can best ensure that the student experience and voice are accurately represented by sharing the student perspective upward to the leadership, communicating it across divisions, and funneling information downward to the students for their ongoing feedback and input. This approach requires the AVP to simultaneously lead and manage both vertically and horizontally across the institution.

Leading and Managing

Research within the corporate sector regarding chief executive officers (CEOs) and their relationship with chief operating officers (COO) can be translated to the VPSA–AVP relationship (Bennett & Miles, 2006; Hytner, 2014; Walton, 2012). Some of this research delves into whether the CEO (i.e., the VPSA) wants the COO (i.e., the AVP) to be a leader or a manager.

Although sometimes used synomously, leadership and management are not the same functions in an organization or a student affairs division. Taylor (2007) contended that "to be a good manager, one must be an effective leader" (p. 130). She also explained that management is more about technical details, whereas leadership is the skillset for dealing with people. Mastering both management and leadership plays an important role in accomplishing the organization's goals.

If VPSAs want AVPs to serve as leaders, then they expect help charting the course and setting the direction; they may expect a sense of partnership. This partnership does not imply an equitable authority, but rather a sense of ownership and accountability. In contrast, many VPSAs prefer a key manager. Managers focus on implementing the vision and strategy the VPSA has already crafted. Both roles are vital—the objective is to align yourself with what your VPSA wants or needs. How much of a leadership role does your VPSA take and how does he or she respond to your attempts at direct leadership. If the VPSA energetically pursues the vision and strategy without inviting the AVP into the process, then the leadership lines are clear (Bennett & Miles, 2006).

Atkins (2010) noted that a good balance of leadership and management engenders a successful strategic planning process. The AVP must allow for in-depth discussion of critical and difficult topics facing the institution while keeping people on task, motivated, and engaged throughout the process (Atkins 2010). Kloppenberg (2004) also discussed the need to balance patience and progress, by sharing information in order to build common ground, yet maintaining momentum and advancing the work. In the end, as noted by Cherrey and Clark (2010),

Colleague input is greatly needed from every perspective in order to put forth and adopt a plan that everyone can commit to for several years out. They must visualize themselves in the plan, making it part of their day-to-day work in order for action to occur. Ultimately the implementation piece of the plan will have the investment, buy-in, innovation, and energy needed to advance initiatives. (p. 82)

Conclusion

The AVP role is complex in nature and falls distinctly in the middle of the administrative hierarchy. It is best defined as a conduit between senior leadership, whose focus is the overall strategic vision for the institution, and those overseeing the functional units within the division. The success of an AVP depends on the ability to strike a balance between leadership and management, while effectively establishing and navigating relationships across the institution and understanding roles and styles as they relate to the VPSA. These skills are critical for the AVP to provide leadership within the strategic planning process, which requires a constant blend of both institutional and functional perspectives. Leading vertically and horizontally from this unique position, the AVP is able to represent multiple constituencies, including the student voice, and successfully translate strategy into results, thereby contributing to the overall success and future direction of the institution.

References

American College Personnel Association and National Association of Student Personnel Administrators. (2015). *Professional competency areas for student affairs educators*. Retrieved from http://www.naspa.org/images/uploads/main/ACPA_NASPA_Professional_Competencies_FINAL.pdf

Atkins, K. (2010). Strategically planning to change. In S. E. Ellis (Ed.), *Special issue: Strategic planning in student affairs* (New Directions for Student Services, No. 132, pp. 17–25). San Francisco, CA: Jossey-Bass.

Bennett, N., & Miles, S. A. (2006, April). Second in command: The misunderstood role of the chief operating officer. *Harvard Business Review*. Retrieved from: https://hbr.org/2006/05/second-in-command-the-misunderstood-role-of-the-chief-operating-officer

Birnbaum, R. (1988). *How colleges work: The cybernetics of academic organization and leadership*. San Francisco, CA: Jossey-Bass.

Cherrey, C., & Clark, E. C. (2010). Strategic planning: Renewal and redesign during turbulent times. In S. E. Ellis (Ed.), *Special issue: Strategic planning in student affairs* (New Directions for Student Services, No. 132, pp. 75–85). San Francisco, CA: Jossey-Bass.

Conneely, J. (2010). Strategic planning and financial management. In S. E. Ellis (Ed.), *Special issue: Strategic planning in student affairs* (New Directions for Student Services, No. 132, pp. 51–61). San Francisco, CA: Jossey-Bass.

Ellis, S. E. (2010). Editor's notes. In S. E. Ellis (Ed.), *Special issue: Strategic planning in student affairs* (New Directions for Student Services, No. 132, pp. 1–4). San Francisco, CA: Jossey-Bass.

French, J., & Raven, B. (1959). The bases of social power. In D. Cartwright (Ed.), *Studies in social power* (pp. 150–167). Ann Arbor, MI: Institute for Social Research.

Harry S. Truman Biography. (n.d.). Retrieved from http://www.biography.com/people/harry-s-truman-9511121

Heffernan, E. T. (2011). Competencies for the seasoned senior student affairs officer. In G. J. Dungy & S. E. Ellis (Eds.), *Exceptional senior student affairs administrators' leadership: Strategies and competencies for success* (pp. 117–120). Washington, DC: National Association of Student Personnel Administrators.

Huy, Q. H. (2001). In praise of middle managers. *Harvard Business Review, 79*(8), 72–81.

Hytner, R. (2014). *Consiglieri: Leading from the shadows*. London, England: Profile Books.

Keeling, R. (Ed.). (2004). *Learning reconsidered*. Washington, DC: American College Personnel Association and National Association of Student Personnel Administrators.

Kloppenberg, L. A. (2004). The balancing act: Leadership in strategic planning. *University of Toledo Law Review, 36*, 103–110.

Kotler, P., & Murphy, P. E. (1981). Strategic planning for higher education. *Journal of Higher Education, 52*(5), 470–489.

Levinson, H., Humphrey, J., Evans, D., & Berry, J. K. (1993). Between CEO and COO. *The Academy of Management Executive, 7*(2), 71–83.

Mills, D. B. (2009). Middle managers: Roles and responsibilities spanning the student affairs career. In G. S. McClellan & J. Stringer (Eds.), *The handbook of student affairs administration* (3rd ed., pp. 355–370). San Francisco, CA: Jossey-Bass.

Northhouse, P. G. (2007). *Leadership theory and practice*. Thousand Oaks, CA: Sage.

Reisser, L., & Roper, L. D. (1999). Using resources to achieve institutional missions and goals. In G. S. Blimling & E. J. Whitt (Eds.), *Good practice in student affairs* (pp. 113–131). San Francisco, CA: Jossey-Bass.

Roper, L. (2002). Relationships: The critical ties that bind professionals. In J. C. Dalton & M. McClinton (Eds.), *Special issue: The art and practical wisdom of student affairs* (New Directions for Student Services, No. 98, pp. 11–26). San Francisco, CA: Jossey-Bass.

Scheuermann, T. S. (2011). Dynamics of supervision. In L. Roper (Ed.), *Special issue: Supporting and supervising mid-level professionals* (New Directions for Student Services, No. 136, pp. 5–16). San Francisco, CA: Jossey-Bass.

Taylor, C. M. (2007). Leading from the middle. In R. L. Ackerman (Ed.), *The mid-level manager in student affairs: Strategies for success* (pp. 127–153). Washington, DC: National Association of Student Personnel Administrators.

Walton, A. G. (2012, June 26). *Move over, CEOs: Why the second-in-command may be the secret to success* [Blog post]. *Forbes*. Retrieved from http://www.forbes.com/sites/alicegwalton/2012/06/26/move-over-ceos-why-the-second-in-command-may-be-the-secret-to-success/

Welsh, J. F., Nunez, W. J., & Petrosko, J. (2005). Faculty and administrative support for strategic planning: A comparison of two- and four-year institutions. *Community College Review, 32*, 20–22.

Wesaw, A. J., & Sponsler, B. A. (2014). *The chief student affairs officer: Responsibilities, opinions, and professional pathways of leaders in student affairs*. Washington, DC: National Association of Student Personnel Administrators.

Whitney, R. (2010). Involving academic faculty in developing and implementing a strategic plan. In S. E. Ellis (Ed.), *Special issue: Strategic planning in student affairs* (New Directions for Student Services, No. 132, pp. 63–74). San Francisco, CA: Jossey-Bass.

Winston, R. B., & Creamer, D. G. (1997). *Improving staffing practices in student affairs*. San Francisco, CA: Jossey-Bass.

Navigating the Politics

Jeanna Mastrodicasa

Politics is present in all organizations, including higher education. Vice presidents for student affairs (VPSAs) report that navigating politics is one of the most challenging issues facing them in their leadership role, but these skills are not taught in graduate programs (Herdlein, 2004; McClellan, 2013). Reisser and Roper (1999) noted that good practice in student affairs requires an individual to develop approaches that are specific to the situation on that campus, including political context. This chapter reviews the basic concepts of politics, applies them to higher education, and offers recommendations to the associate/assistant vice president (AVP) to navigate political issues successfully.

Higher Education and Politics

Viewed as simply the study of influence, applicable to all organizations, politics is inevitable (Bogue, 2007). Morgan (2006) suggested that even though many see politics as unpleasant, it is an essential aspect of organizational life—it's the use of negotiation and consultation between individuals to settle differences. When we examine the relationship between interests, conflict, and power, the act of resolving the individual differences of people who are part of an organization is what makes the organization work (Morgan, 2006). Nevertheless, politics causes apprehension among many student affairs professionals. As applied to student affairs, Ellis and Moon (1991) stated,

> It is traditional for the helping professional to maintain distance from political processes and activities on campus. Being political may feel unethical and contradictory because it is often seen as manipulative. . . . They have not been encouraged or rewarded for being political. (p. 49)

By their very nature, colleges and universities are political institutions (Hecht, Pina, & Rue, 2015). Appleton (1991) ascribed the complexity of a higher education institution to the often-conflicting interests of its vast range of stakeholders: faculty, students, staff, alumni, parents and families, community members, donors, and governmental agencies. Appleton's viewpoint that a student affairs professional's power is limited is a bit outdated—today, the incredible focus on student-related issues positions the student affairs professional as the expert. Further, AVPs see clearly the wide range of stakeholders' viewpoints because of the middle-manager function of the position; they have a sophisticated understanding of how such interests and expectations interact; and they know how to respond to those interests and expectations in a timely and productive manner (Ellis & Moon, 1991).

Creating a visual diagram of people and relationships clarifies the politics of an organization. McCaffery (2010) recommended analyzing your profile of political resources, comparing it to others with whom you might interact, and drawing up an action plan to understand your political potential. Stringer (2009) recommended constructing a political map to visually depict the political terrain to see how you influence others or how you can be influenced. Stringer used the example of a VPSA to map out a concentric circle showing those stakeholders who have daily, regular, or periodic contact or access, which is also relevant to an AVP (see Figure 5.1).

Figure 5.1. Political Map of a Senior Student Affairs Officer

Note. Adapted from "The Political Environment of the Student Affairs Administrator," by J. Stringer, 2009. In G. S. McClellan & J. Stringer (Eds.), *The Handbook of Student Affairs Administration* (3rd ed., p. 432), San Francisco, CA: Jossey-Bass. Reprinted with permission.

Power

McCaffery (2010) described power as "an inescapable feature of organizational life" (p. 315) and encouraged managers to make the most of their political resources. To be successful, you should maximize your power to advance the interests of the department, the institution, and yourself. Power comes from: (a) a formal position or role; (b) personal authority, including personal characteristics that others find attractive, influential, or persuasive; (c) expertise, both real and imagined; (d) access to information; and (e) the ability to recognize and seize an opportunity to be in the right place at the right time (McCaffery, 2010; Morgan, 2006).

Birnbaum (1988) defined power as "the ability to produce intended change in others, so that they will be more likely to act in accord with your own preferences" (p. 13). Power takes on several forms—coercive power, expert power, and referent power—in all fields, including higher education (French & Raven, 1968), as well as the control of scarce resources, technology, the informal organization, and collegiality (Morgan, 2006). Those who hold the power in organizations can make things happen; further, because individuals need things from one another, power relationships are multidirectional (Bolman & Deal, 2008).

Conflict

Morgan (2006) defined interests as the reasons a person acts—goals, values, desires, expectations, or other inclinations. Viewing your own interests as an area you want to protect, achieve, preserve, or increase, you defend those interests when they are encroached on or attacked. Conflict arises when interests collide. Organizational conflict is often viewed as a negative or dysfunctional force. However, conflict can also allow the best ideas to advance when guided through robust dialogue. Morgan (2006) stated that conflict, always present in organizations, comes from a variety of sources: personal; interpersonal; group rivalry; a scarcity of resources; and structures, roles, attitudes, and stereotypes built into an organization. Bogue (2007) portrayed the creation of conflict from a positive viewpoint, as a way to "test ideas and beliefs, and a means for developing identity and self-understanding" (p. 41). He argued that conflict is a way to make a leader stronger and is an "essential instrument of apprehending truth" (p. 41).

The scarcity of resources in higher education often fuels organizational conflict. In times of plentiful resources, there is less conflict, because programs and facilities receive their funds. In leaner times, however, conflict arises when individuals compete for jobs, titles, and prestige; departments compete for resources and power; and groups compete for control over policy decisions. Conflict is particularly likely to occur where departments or groups intersect; by the very nature of being different, groups or departments have some differences in interests or perspectives, which may lead to conflict. The challenge is to recognize and manage that conflict so that it is productive (Bolman & Deal, 2008).

Managing Conflict

Bogue (2007) asserted that leaders of higher education institutions have three basic responsibilities in managing conflicts: preventing unnecessary conflict, resolving conflict, and creating conflict. To prevent unnecessary conflict, Bogue recommended that leaders first create a set of organizational values and a mission statement to give basic guidance to the entire organization. Second, Bogue suggested resolving conflicts through (a) finding win–win options, (b) bringing in a third party to help mediate between two ideas, and (c) negotiating to make it work. Finally, a leader should create conflict to test values and priorities, as well as encourage open, honest dialogue.

To illustrate how AVPs can apply Bogue's (2007) three basic responsibilities to manage conflict productively, consider the following scenario:

> *Hern State University's student affairs division has historically struggled with limited resources and an ambitious staff. Departmental directors frequently propose adding new services or programs without additional resources to support these ideas, and rarely propose stopping others. As they do more with less, their staff are burned out and are less willing to collaborate with each other. Meanwhile, their leadership team, led by the AVP, created the division's strategic plan, which added some written guidance for its goals, vision, and mission. Accordingly, having this document as the compass for new goals and assessing the impact of programs and services has prevented unnecessary conflicts and resolved others. Some conflicts can't be resolved easily; negotiation skills and an outside facilitator during retreats have helped to reduce conflict and find common wins.*

Managing conflict is a key skill an AVP must use to navigate politics. Bogue (2007) set forth five principles of managing conflicts:

- **Confrontation:** Look conflict in the eye and avoid third-party conversations. Get the differences on the table.
- **Communication:** Make inquiries and insure that you have all facts and feelings relative to a conflict.
- **Compassion:** Don't make enemies of or demonize dissenters. You cannot hope that colleagues will give you the truth of your organization if they fear your reprisal or degradation.
- **Cooperation:** Separate people from issues where possible.
- **Creation:** Look for invention as a means of generating win-win or integrative solutions to conflicts before you escalate the conflict forum and lose decision discretion. (p. 42)

Finally, AVPs must spend time knowing themselves in order to lead by example (Hands & Pina, 2014). Whether it is through various diagnostic processes, such as the Myers-Briggs Type Indicator or Gallup's StrengthsFinder, AVPs should understand their own best attributes as well as which skills complement them. For many aspects of the job, AVPs work in committees. That's where they can use the knowledge of their individual strengths, rather than mere positional authority, to build teams. Cabellon and Klotz (2015) reviewed the importance of understanding how you are perceived by others, how others see and feel about you; those perceptions influence the way you fit into the organizational culture. Your professional reputation is based on accomplishments and your likeability, and both matter in building a professional network.

Being Successful in the Political Realm

Having a positive approach to politics is essential for an AVP to be successful. Hecht et al. (2015) outlined three steps to building relationships and allowing decisions to evolve as the situation demands, without letting the conflict drive apart the parties: (a) listen, understand, and respect differences; (b) look for mutual gains; and (c) stay alert to system dynamics to take new leadership stands. Political issues arise from differences of opinion, but each opinion deserves understanding and respect while the parties build a consensus of some kind. Hopefully, each party gains something to move the discussion forward. Such respect truly can make the difference in keeping things positive during a political conflict and sets up the leader's ability to make different decisions when the issues shift.

Hands and Pina (2014) presented a list of recommendations for navigating campus politics: (a) fully understand the culture and the process of allocating resources on your campus; (b) invest in communication; (c) align needs and values; and (d) be patient and persistent. Resources are the central issue in political conflicts and knowing the full process, the nuances, and the players in the allocation of those resources on campus is crucial to effectively managing them. Additionally, the ability to articulate the needs and values of the organization and to match them with resources is crucial to being a credible leader. Finally, skills such as communication, patience, and persistence support a successful AVP through political conflicts on campus.

As presenters at the NASPA AVP Institute, Hands and Pina (2014) and Hecht et al. (2015) set forth several specific ways AVPs can demonstrate strengths in a political framework: resourcefulness; a problem-solving approach; the ability to creatively maximize resources; the knowledge of and expertise in the student experience and college students in general; a collaborative approach to problems; and connections to the larger environment at a higher education institution, including career networks, parents, active alumni, and more.

To navigate politics, AVPs should master the "four knows": know your environment, know your university, know your department, and know yourself. The environment of higher education and the focus on mission, accountability, and its role in social change all provide context for decisions to be made by the institution, student affairs, and the AVP (McCaffery, 2010). Accordingly, an AVP needs to be connected and committed to understanding these aspects to successfully advocate and position the organization. This knowledge helps frame new ideas, shape advocacy efforts, and align common goals to reduce potential conflict and increase support.

Knowing the institution is a crucial part of serving in excellence as an AVP. The governance of the institution can be complex, and understanding the role of the governing board versus the management of the institution as well as processes and concepts of shared governance is part of knowing who holds the authority for making decisions at various levels. Knowing the university's mission, strategic plan, central goals, and its path forward is important to understanding the big picture and where student affairs fits in the larger environment (McCaffery, 2010). Klawitter (2015) recommended knowing the big ideas at an institution of higher education and identifying the people behind them. He described big ideas as those that can provide a transformational opportunity for the organization to grow or advance and are commonly included in strategic plans, annual reports, and websites.

Case Study

To help readers understand the complexity of navigating politics as an AVP, four seasoned sitting AVPs were asked to share how they would respond to a political case study.

> *Within the division of student affairs at Peaches College, budget cuts over the past few years have reduced staff numbers. The dean of students office changed its scope to include the responsibilities historically carried out by the health promotions staff and student activities but did not discuss this change with either the vice president or the staff of either of the other departments. All these departments report to the VPSA, not to the AVP, but the two aggrieved departments complained to the AVP.*
>
> *The VPSA was happy to have the work completed and found that the work was done quicker and with more robust results, but did not address the shift in scope with any of the departments. A year later, the dean of students asked for additional staff and successfully justified the request by pointing to the new scope of responsibilities. As a result, two departments are now pitted against the third. The staff feel resentful regarding the scarce resources, they are distrustful of the other department, and the interpersonal relationships are conflictive.*

Recommendations:

- o Determine which aspects of the assignment can be successfully completed by each department so staff feel some ownership and contribution to the high-profile task. This is an opportunity to find a win–win situation for the parties, while helping them to see the perspectives of the others.

- Use the guiding principles of the division of student affairs and the departments by examining their missions, values, and goals. Are there inherent conflicts as they are written or practiced? Are departments going beyond their scope?
- Examine data regarding resources and assessment. Are the departments producing the desired outcomes with their resources? This is important for knowing your organization and for actually using the data that you collect to make decisions.
- Have a general discussion about the need for clarity of roles and responsibilities at the leadership team meeting or retreat. Knowing which department or individual is responsible for what task reduces duplicate work and competition for assignments. An outside facilitator may be needed to keep the discussion on task.

Conclusion

Overall, the AVP must navigate the politics up, down, and across the organization and be able to build connections in each situation. Developing those skills takes experience, and opportunities to practice those skills can only enhance the results. Politics is often cited as one of the greatest challenges for AVPs, regardless of their length of experience. It can often be the determining factor in a person's success in the position. An AVP who better understands the organization, the department, and the players—as well as personal strengths—is much more likely to be successful in navigating the politics of any situation.

References

Appleton, J. R. (1991). The context. In P. L. Moore (Ed.), *Managing the political dimension of student affairs* (New Directions for Student Services, No. 55, pp. 5–15). San Francisco, CA: Jossey-Bass.

Birnbaum, R. (1988). *How colleges work: The cybernetics of academic organization and leadership*. San Francisco, CA: Jossey-Bass.

Bogue, E. G. (2007). *Leadership legacy moments: Visions and values for stewards of collegiate mission*. Westport, CT: Praeger.

Bolman, L. G., & Deal, T. E. (2008). *Reframing organizations: Artistry, choice, and leadership* (4th ed.). San Francisco, CA: Jossey-Bass.

Cabellon, E., & Klotz, A. M. (2015, January 29). Unwritten rules of student affairs [Blog post]. Retrieved from http://lizgross.net/unwritten-rules-student-affairs

Ellis, H., & Moon, J. (1991). The middle manager: Truly in the middle. In P. L. Moore (Ed.), *Managing the political dimension of student affairs* (New Directions for Student Services, No. 55, pp. 17–26). San Francisco, CA: Jossey-Bass.

French, J. R. P., Jr., & Raven, B. (1968). The bases of social power. In D. Cartwright & A. Zander (Eds.), *Group dynamics: Research and theory* (3rd ed., pp. 259–269). New York, NY: Harper & Row.

Hands, A., & Pina, J. (2014, January). *Institutional politics and effective leadership*. Paper presented at NASPA AVP Institute, New Orleans, LA.

Hecht, A., Pina, J., & Rue, P. (2015, January). *Institutional politics and effective leadership*. Paper presented at NASPA AVP Institute, Long Beach, CA.

Herdlein, R. J. (2004). Survey of chief student affairs officers regarding relevance of graduate preparation of new professionals. *NASPA Journal, 42*(1), 51–71.

Klawitter, M. (2015, January 24). Know your university [Blog post]. Retrieved from http://lizgross.net/know-university

McCaffery, P. (2010). *The higher education manager's handbook: Effective leadership and management in universities and colleges* (2nd ed.). New York, NY: Routledge.

McClellan, G. S. (2013, March 11). Things I didn't learn in graduate school [Blog post]. Retrieved from http://chronicle.com/article/Things-I-Didnt-Learn-in/137807/#disqus_thread

Morgan, G. (2006). *Images of organization* (3rd ed.). London, England: Sage.

Reisser, L., & Roper, L. D. (1999). Using resources to achieve institutional missions and goals. In G. S. Blimling & E. J. Whitt (Eds.), *Good practice in student affairs: Principles to foster student learning* (pp. 113–131). San Francisco, CA: Jossey-Bass.

Stringer, J. (2009). The political environment of the student affairs administrator. In G. S. McClellan & J. Stringer (Eds.), *The handbook of student affairs administration* (3rd ed., pp. 425–446). San Francisco, CA: Jossey-Bass.

Human Resource Management

Julie Payne-Kirchmeier

Justina, an assistant vice president (AVP) in the student affairs division at Midwestern State University, is walking through the student union when she is approached by Martin, one of the directors she supervises. Martin, who oversees dining operations, is visibly angry and upset. Martin says, "I'm really frustrated. My staff just told me that you made a change to the food line operation yesterday, and you didn't tell me. How am I supposed to do my job if I don't know what's going on?" Justina is a former director of food services. She explains that she felt it was a customer service issue that needed to be handled right then. Martin says, "But I'm the director of dining, not you. I'm just not sure what my role is." Justina says they can discuss it more at their one-on-one that afternoon and leaves to go to a meeting with her boss, the vice president for student affairs (VPSA).

During the meeting, the VPSA says, "I'm concerned about the lack of oversight in our recreation center. I know the director, Sam, reports to you, but what's going on there? They don't seem to be in step with what we're trying to do as a division and are not in alignment with our strategic plan. And when is Sam actually in her office anyway?" Justina is confused and feels like she can't win. In one arena, she's too deep in the weeds. In the other, she's not involved enough. As a supervisor in this AVP role, what is she expected to do?

AVPs face situations like this all the time. The nature of the AVP role is ambiguous, shifting, and nebulous at best. Priorities are constantly shifting, and AVPs are expected to maneuver seamlessly between detail and direction. Often they oversee areas that have highly competent, content-specific leadership and are expected to understand a myriad of competing priorities, issues, and competencies. What then, is their role as a supervisor?

The American College Personnel Association and National Association of Student Personnel Administrators (2010) joint publication, *Professional Competency Areas for Student Affairs Practitioners*, identifies human and organizational resources as one of the 10 competency areas critical for success in the field of student affairs. Within the narrative of this competency lies supervision and the accompanying skills of selection, motivation, and formal evaluation of staff. Perhaps more than any other group in higher education, student affairs professionals reflect the most diversity in training, background, and experiences (Sandeen & Barr, 2006). As such, supervising such a group of individuals can be challenging, especially at the AVP level, where staff have direct oversight of specific functions of the division. AVPs often find themselves supervising people who have more knowledge about a specific functional area and may have more experience in the field.

How does the AVP navigate this role, one that involves overseeing directors who are content experts in their field while still moving the full team toward the fulfillment of the divisional mission and vision? How does the AVP build a trusting relationship that allows for a free exchange of information, staff development, and critical feedback? This chapter addresses all these questions about supervising and managing as the number two in the student affairs organization. In addition, numerous sitting AVPs offer words of advice for successfully supervising from this unique position.

Importance of Supervision

> *"Supervision can be a place where a living profession breathes and learns." (Hawkins & Shohet, 2007, p. 205)*

Winston and Creamer (1997) defined supervision in higher education as:

A management function intended to promote the achievement of institutional goals and enhance the personal and professional capabilities of staff. Supervision interprets the institutional mission and focuses human and fiscal resources on the promotion of individual and organizational competence. (p. 42)

Because human resources in colleges and universities is viewed as one of the most valuable assets for the organization, working with and helping staff improve via supervision is a critical component of organizational success. Furthermore, supervision in helping professions such as education holds an important place in the training, evaluation, and further growth of a professional's competence within an organizational setting (Squires, 1978). Research indicates that effective supervision of human resources can improve an organization's overall performance as it relates to achievement of goals and outcomes (Hatch & Dyer, 2004). Because the focus in higher education is on development and growth, the primary goal of supervision should be to hire capable, self-directed people and to facilitate their growth and development. Herrick (1977) stated, "If people are viewed as capable of self-direction in an appropriate growth-promoting atmosphere, this perspective may point to supervision as an enabling, facilitating process" (p. 2).

Given the definition and the importance of supervision, the supervisor is clearly one of the most influential roles in higher education. Therefore, supervising effectively is a fundamental component of building organizational and individual capacity, as well as facilitating long-term success for the organization. Simply put, supervision is a crucial skill necessary for all AVPs.

Supervision and Management

> *"Once you hire great people, your job becomes managing them into a winning team." (Welch, 2005, p. 117)*

Supervision is inextricably tied to management within the context of student affairs work. Management can be defined as "the organization and coordination of the activities of a business in order to achieve defined objectives" (Winston & Creamer, 1997, p. 442). Because it also serves as the catchall name for "the director and managers who have the power and responsibility to make decisions and oversee an enterprise" (Winston & Creamer, 1997, p. 442), we can see immediately how management and supervision are coupled. A study by Hatch and Dyer (2004) showed that the effective management of certain human resource activities, including the selection and development of staff, improve an organization's overall performance.

AVPs are often charged with strategy and overseeing strategic processes for a division. In addition, as the number two to the VPSA, the AVP occasionally assumes the duties of the VPSA. In the role, the AVP carries forward the mission and vision of both the VPSA and the division and represents that division not only to the executive team for the institution, but to all direct reports and staff within the division as well. Linking mission and vision to supervision is crucial if AVPs are truly to understand the power of a supervisory relationship.

Finally, AVPs are expected to manage other groups, not just their direct reports. Managing VPSAs and managing side-to-side with peers both in and outside of student affairs also requires a considerable amount of attention. Vijay Pendakur, associate vice president at California State University, Fullerton, stated, "Managing my portfolio is only half the job, as my AVP position is tied to a number of strategic plan objectives that cut across the institution."

Supervision Challenges for AVPs

> "An organization, no matter how well designed, is only as good as the people who live and work in it." (Hock, 2005, p. 42)

Although little has been written about supervising specifically from the AVP role in student affairs, we can look to other positions in higher education for insight, such as middle managers in student affairs, deans of colleges, and associate provost positions—and even chief operating officers (COOs) of corporations. The similarities in the issues faced by these different roles shed light on the challenges that AVPs face in their own supervisory responsibilities.

In the administrative context, "a dean may be called upon to act as persuader, negotiator, or arbitrator, convincing faculty to endorse central administration policy" (Montez, Wolverton, & Gmelch, 2003, p. 241). AVPs face similar issues and perform similar roles for their division and for the departments they oversee. One AVP from a private elite institution, speaking anonymously, stated:

> There are times when I have to convince multiple constituencies—faculty, students, administrators, parents, alumni, and community members—that the direction of the university administration is the best possible approach to take. These are often difficult moments, but ones in which I am fully aware of my role and responsibility as an agent of my university.

Whether I personally agree with the decision or policy, I work for the university and my job is to get them all on board.

In their work, Montez et al. (2003) found that deans often struggle with role conflict. Deans get "caught between faculty and administration, between students and faculty, or between administration and public," and the dean is expected to "advocate for opposing sides of issues" in these instances (p. 243). These pressures and situations are similar to what an AVP contends with. AVPs may find themselves at odds with an administrative decision, at the center of competing priorities within their own unit, or having to explain and advocate for different perspectives.

Wayne Young, Jr., associate vice president for student life at Creighton University, stated that "an AVP may supervise several directors—and often those directors have agenda items that may be in competition with one another. Often the trick in this scenario is to help the individual directors see the congruence of their agendas." This refocusing on larger priorities and areas of overlap is one method AVPs can use to bring a sense of common ground back to a situation. Cynthia Hernandez, assistant vice president for student affairs at Texas A&M University, summed it up this way: "In being an advocate for my departments, I also keep the needs of the entire division in mind. Moving the division toward its goals, in alignment with the university's goals, is of the utmost importance."

Role ambiguity, or confusion about expectations related to positional pressures, is another issue faced by deans and AVPs alike. Sometimes information about the scope and responsibility of a job is inadequate, unavailable, or contradictory (Montez et al., 2003). Clear expectations are not always possible. Changing and shifting priorities, external influences on different department or divisional programs, and unforeseen issues cause the landscape for the AVP to continually shift, and that of their direct reports as well. The AVP needs to navigate this ambiguity by figuring out key directions and making appropriate decisions on behalf of the division. Supervising from this frame becomes challenging, because the AVPs may be unable to give clear expectations to their direct reports if they themselves do not have clear direction.

Consider now the challenges faced by a midlevel manager in student affairs. Although not as experienced as most AVPs, these professionals—rarely directly responsible for the overall goals of their department—nonetheless often find themselves facing role ambiguity. Like these midlevel managers, AVPs do not have the ultimate responsibility for the direction of the student affairs division, but they are expected to understand the long-range vision, share this with direct reports and multiple constituency groups, and balance competing priorities within shifting environments. Lori Stettler, assistant vice chancellor at Southern Illinois University, stated:

> Some days, I feel like a leader. Other days, I feel as though I'm right back to being in middle management—caught in between the needs of my staff and students, and the vision of my VC [vice chancellor] or direction of the division. The skills I learned in my role as a middle manager in a department are resurfacing now, but at a higher level.

Another position within academia comparable to an AVP position in student affairs is the associate provost role. In the position descriptions for associate provost responsibilities on Vitae, *The Chronicle of Higher Education's* online job board (https://chroniclevitae.com/job_search/new), each description—regardless of institution type—has supervision as part of the requirement. The associate provost role is similar in scope and challenge to the dean position, albeit with less of a direct curriculum connection (unless specifically stated in the job description). However, the supervisory skills necessary for this position are similar to that of a dean, because they, too, are not coordinating a specific function and have multiple stakeholder considerations they must balance and prioritize.

The corporate environment offers perspective on supervisory expectations for AVPs as the number twos. One comparative role is a COO. Bennett and Miles (2006) explained that COO supervision must shift away from direct oversight and day-to-day operations: "A COO must be able to direct and coach others throughout the business" (p. 6). Steven Reinemund, former chairman and CEO at PespsiCo who was promoted to COO, told Bennett and Miles (2006) that the COO role "requires an individual who can step out of doing day-to-day, hands-on directing and leading of a business, and direct and teach and coach others" (p. 6). A similar skill set is required of many AVPs who step into the role after coming out of a director-level position overseeing a specific function.

In taking these different roles into account and comparing them to the supervisory expectations of an AVP, we can see very quickly that the demands and expectations for supervision at this level are very different from that for a director. As such, the skills necessary for this position—both from an institution-level perspective and within student affairs—are crucial for success.

Types and Models of Supervision

In order to be a better supervisor, AVPs need to understand the research associated with different types of supervision. These approaches span a multitude of professions, including business, education, social science, government, and not-for-profit organizations (Bennett & Miles, 2006; Kadushin, 1992; Montez et al., 2003; Winston & Creamer, 1999). Because institutions of higher education are astoundingly complex and involved, they tend to use a combination of supervisory approaches within the organization, especially given the different relationships and roles possessed by individuals within the college or university community.

Student affairs work, as evidenced through our student development theory research, is firmly rooted in the social sciences. Within the literature there are several approaches to supervision, some of which involve "clients" (in student affairs work, these would be our students); in others the supervisory role takes on more of a management focus—one with a more direct connection of supervisor to supervisee.

The models of supervision fall into one of four predominant forms of supervision: psychotherapy based, developmental, integrative, and synergistic (Bernard & Goodyear, 1998). A psychotherapy-based model in its purest form is generally more suited toward counseling and therapeutic relationships, because they involve client-based supervision. However, some researchers have used the principles of psychotherapy to develop models that include person-centered supervision, feminist models of supervision, and cognitive–behavioral supervision. These are beneficial when supervising staff with a wide range of backgrounds and experiences.

Developmental models, as the name suggests, incorporate a process by which the supervisee moves through a series of stages that are qualitatively different from one another, each stage resulting in the culmination of specific characteristics or skills (Chagon & Russell, 1995). This type of supervision is also strongly relational and collegial, something crucial to student affairs work (Littrel, Lee-Borden, & Lorenz, 1979). Several of these developmental models exist for supervision in human service and education work, but all involve the supervisee progressing through stages. Student affairs professionals often find themselves using a developmental approach, particularly when working through performance evaluations and professional development planning with a staff member.

The integrated development model, or IDM, developed by Stoltenberg (1981) outlines levels of development having a direct correlation to a supervisee's experience and comfort level with his or her roles. This type of supervision requires supervisors to fully understand the strengths and limitations of each staff member. Supervisors using this model need to leverage skills and approaches that correspond to the level of the supervisee's readiness, much like Sanford's (1962) challenge and support model of student development. Often, this model is leveraged from one of two vantage points—a strengths-based philosophy (Hodges & Clifton, 2004) or a deficit-based one, in which the supervisor attempts to address weaknesses in a staff member's skill set. Additional models that are in the integrated category include Bernard's (1979) discrimination model, in which distinct focus areas are identified and discussed, and the systems approach to supervision, in which supervisor and supervisee develop a mutually evolving, power-sharing relationship (Holloway, 1995).

One model of supervision that draws heavily on an integrated framework is Kadushin's (1992) discussion of supervision. Kadushin began by reflecting on a very early work by Dawson (1926), in which Dawson broke down supervision into three distinct areas: administrative, educational, and supportive. The administrative frame concerns the promotion and maintenance of good standards of work and coordination of policies and practices. The educational frame focuses on each individual staff member and his or her development, and the supportive frame focuses on developing and maintaining relationships and cultivating a positive work environment. Although later works discussed an evolution on these frames as they relate to a learning organization such as higher education (Kadushin, 1992; Salaman, 1995) and sought to incorporate and involve the management lens into the model (Drucker, 1988; Salaman, 1995), these three categories can be helpful for AVPs as they move through developing their own framework for supervision.

Most recently, student affairs as a profession appears to have adopted more synergistic approaches to staff supervision, an evolution of the integrated models just mentioned. Synergistic staff supervision is focused on a more holistic approach, allowing supervisors the ability to clarify expectations through discussion of performance and informal appraisals (Winston & Creamer, 1997). This type of supervision, which also takes into account the institutional culture and external environment in which the institution is located, involves five areas:

- discussion of exemplary performance,
- discussion of long-term career goals,
- discussion of inadequate performance,
- frequency of informal performance appraisals, and
- discussion of personal attitudes. (Winston & Creamer, 1997, pp. 42–43)

This approach enhances the personal and professional development of professional staff and is one that allows for a balance between empowerment and accountability by establishing open lines of communication, supervisory feedback and appraisal, identification of long-term career goals, and joint identification of critical knowledge and skills necessary for success and advancement (Winston & Creamer, 1999). This type of supervision encourages and builds an environment of trust.

Although understanding these key types of supervisory models is important, what specific areas do AVPs need to better understand as they relate to supervision in this unique role? How should AVPs best approach this process? Often, student affairs staff are not as intentional about developing a supervisory framework, nor do they take the time to fully understand and identify their own supervisory expectations and styles. The following section discusses skills and approaches necessary for AVPs to be effective supervisors at the senior student affairs officer level.

AVP Supervision and Management

> *"Supervision is an opportunity to bring someone back to their own mind, to show them how good they can be." (Kline, 2015, p. 119)*

Approaching supervision as an AVP can be a daunting task. Recall the scenario at the beginning of this chapter. Justina was faced with a challenge of supervision often expressed by AVPs. How do AVPs know when to get into key details and when to stay at a strategic level? How do they let go of their content-expert areas so that those in charge of those programs feel empowered? AVPs sometimes feel like a "ping-pong ball," a "rubber band," or as if they were "stuck in an endless game of tag," as several current AVPs expressed it. Understanding how to successfully develop their teams and supervise director-level staff is a crucial element for a successful AVP.

The remainder of this chapter covers crucial steps and skills AVPs should take to be effective supervisors for their teams. Comments from 15 current AVPs from various institutional types, backgrounds, and experiences support key points along the way. Some of these AVPs chose to remain anonymous; others did not. Their voices and recommendations will help readers better understand how these concepts apply to the AVP role.

Acknowledge That This Supervisory Role is Different

The AVPs included in informal research for this chapter unanimously indicated that moving from a director-level role to an AVP role resulted in a different relationship with direct reports. No longer were they working with midlevel staff who needed more development and challenge in their roles. Pendakur put it this way:

> Although the fundamentals of supervision in student affairs still resonate ... supervising only directors has changed my focus a bit. I no longer spend much or any of my time on developmental supervision; rather I find myself working

alongside my directors to help them think through a planning document, navigate campus politics, or rework a complex budget.

Scott Peska, dean for students at Waubonsee Community College, stated:

> As a director of a unit, I found that I was setting a clear vision, mission, and goals for the department and could set clear expectations to help my team to meet those objectives. As a dean overseeing managers [similar to directors on 4-year campuses], I find that my style of supervision has shifted to one of guidance, support, and to serve as a sounding board to help direct reports understand how their decisions may have broader implications throughout the institution.

As we can see, AVPs generally understand that their role is vastly different in terms of supervision than that of a director or the leader of a specific unit. AVPs need to acknowledge this early on and set appropriate expectations, goals, and relationships with their teams. Additionally, more seasoned AVPs need to continually navigate this space, particularly as it relates to areas in which the AVP has more experience. Finally, for AVPs with dual roles (an AVP role and a focused role, such as a director position), this space becomes even more delicate, because the AVP navigates between two distinct supervisory roles.

Define Your Supervision Philosophy and Approach

Two of the most important things an AVP can do are (a) assess their own supervisory style and approach, and (b) develop a formal supervision philosophy. Several AVPs indicated that writing out a supervisory philosophy can be a great first step in helping direct reports get to know you and what motivates you. Staff members rally around a common philosophy, because it provides purpose and perspective. From a practical frame, it also gives your teams something with which to better understand the AVPs and their leadership and supervisory style. AVPs should perform this exercise as they take on their first AVP position or move from one position to another (e.g., take on a new AVP role or encounter a dramatic shift to their portfolio of responsibility), because supervisory philosophies can change. Creating a philosophy of style and approach involves identifying strengths; preferences in a supervisory role; and tendencies in structuring interactions, communications, development, and planning with the team.

Identify Your Strengths

Winston and Creamer (1997) pointed out the crucial nature of understanding an approach to supervision and how this intentional action on the part of a supervisor can set the stage for success. These researchers developed a short inventory to assess your own style (see http://www.staffingpractices.soe.vt.edu/Library/supinventory.pdf). Other assessments, including the Myers-Briggs Type Indicator, DiSC, and Clifton StrengthsFinder, can help AVPs understand their strengths and how those strengths affect their supervisory approach.

Outline Your Expectations—And Your Quirks

Many of the AVPs surveyed indicated that an AVP should develop a document about themselves to give to their direct reports. This document, which is different from the philosophy document, outlines what the AVP expects from his or her team and what the team can expect from the AVP. The AVP can include any and all pieces of information that a team may need to know about—including communication frequency; transparency; procedures when staff have an issue they cannot resolve; notification of critical events; and even small things like quirks, pet peeves, and so on. Prepared as a list, such a document also serves as a fantastic "get to know me" activity for the team. One AVP stated:

> I developed this document by crowdsourcing information from people I supervised in the past. It was amazing the things that they came up with, and I was astonished at just how accurate the information incorporated

truly was. My new team found the list invaluable and has begun to add things to it as we navigate our supervisory relationship.

Two of the AVPs interviewed recommended creating a document like this for two groups: one for any administrative support staff that have specific roles and tasks associated with managing the AVPs (and their schedules) and one for direct reports. The expectations will most likely be different.

AVPs might also consider using one of the supervisory approaches or models discussed previously in this chapter to fully develop a supervisory philosophy and framework. From something as relatively simple as Kadushin's (1992) administrative, educational, and supportive frames to the more complex synergistic frame offered by Winston and Creamer (1997), bringing structure to a supervisory approach is a proven method by which many AVPs have been able to help teams understand their perspective, direction, and expectations.

Learn the Culture of the Organization and Institution

The culture of the organization and the institution in which an organization is housed can have significant impact on the operation, direction, and oversight necessary for the organization to be successful. Therefore, AVPs cannot overlook the importance of learning the culture of their organization (or division) and the institution of which they are a part. To navigate how a particular division and institution perceive the role of supervision and management on campus, AVPs should keep the following suggestions in mind.

Listen More Than You Talk

From a management and a supervisory lens, there is nothing more important than listening to faculty, staff, colleagues, students, alumni, and other stakeholders about the institution and the organization. These perspectives can provide an AVP critical insight into how the university feels about supervisory issues such accountability, notification, and so on. Willie Banks, interim assistant vice president for student affairs at Cleveland State University, described this quite succinctly. When asked what advice he had for AVPs, he said, "Listen, listen, listen, and then get out of the way."

Maintain a Mission-focused Approach

Many AVPs keep both individual staff members and their collective team focused by connecting the activities and behaviors of individuals within the unit or division to the larger divisional and institutional missions. This connection helps manage competing priorities between individuals on the team when they arise. Young said,

> An AVP may supervise several directors, and often these directors have agenda items that may be in competition with one another. Always, always, always keep the focus on students and their learning. If you want a comment of support or critique, start and end with what students would need or expect.

Peska further stated, "In regard to vision and planning, my role has shifted to helping my direct reports shape their goals and mission to ensure they align with that of the institution and the direction of our division." Kimberly M. Ferguson, dean of students at Spelman College, agreed, saying, "The success of my role is highly dependent on my ability to work collaboratively with others to find the middle ground that meets the needs of the institution and the students we serve." Finally, Hernandez stated, "In being an advocate for my departments, I also keep the needs of the entire division in mind. Moving the division toward its goals, in alignment with the university's goals, is of utmost importance." These perspectives adhere to mission and purpose, underscoring the importance of an AVP in helping direct reports understand how their actions affect the long-term direction of the institution and, particularly, the students.

Develop a Relationship with Human Resources

"One of the most important relationships I have is with my primary divisional contact in human resources," said one AVP. Indeed, this is a crucial relationship for any AVP to foster—both for the AVP's supervisory needs and for those of their direct reports. Information about human resources policy, hiring practices, accountability measures, affirmative action, benefits, payroll, and other issues related to supervision are things your human resources representatives know quite well, and they can serve as a powerful advocate for you concerning a supervisory issue that you need to address quickly.

Some divisions have a lead person on staff who is responsible for all human resources paperwork and processes. This staff member can end up being the primary conduit to human resources on the AVP's behalf. Understanding the organization and culture is critical: By connecting with this person, an AVP quickly learns when to go directly to human resources and when to stick with their divisional contact.

Know Your VPSA's Expectations

There is no more important relationship to an AVP than the one with the VPSA. This pairing needs to be strong and rooted in trust and openness; both parties should feel equally able to speak freely with each other. Ideally, the AVP has a strong understanding of the VPSA's vision, and the VPSA has a strong, strategic partner in which to openly share ideas for discussion and debate. In short, a positive pairing here spells success for the division; a negative one spells disaster. However, in order for AVPs to effectively supervise and manage, they need to fully understand the expectations their VPSAs have for them and work hard to curate this relationship.

Understand the VPSA's Expectations for Your Role

AVP portfolios or roles are not standardized in our field. These positions are created for a wide variety of reasons. For some, the AVP is expected to be front facing, interacting regularly with students. For others, the role is operational and administrative. Still, for others, it is primarily a strategic role, designed to assist the VPSA to accomplish the vision for the division. Finally, other AVPs have portfolios that combine these different functions. Due to the unique nature and structure of each AVP role, communicating frequently with the VPSA about role clarity and expectations is important. For a new AVP, having a direct conversation early on with the VPSA about expectations for the AVP and the role, coupled with a clearly written job description and understanding of the VPSA's vision, allows the AVP to better manage his or her own team. For AVPs with more experience, these continued conversations allow for changes in the landscape to be better understood and incorporated into expectations for the role.

Develop Your Own "VPSA 101"

It is not enough to understand the VPSA's expectations. AVPs must also understand the needs and workings of their VPSAs. These are not always obvious; it takes time for the AVP and VPSA to navigate the development of their own partnership. For example, how does the VPSA like to be reached in times of crisis? How comfortable is the VPSA with social media? Is the VPSA better at in-person communication or written communication? What matters does the VPSA want to be updated on immediately, and in what manner, and what information is of less interest? These details are not written down, but they nevertheless have a direct impact on the supervisory relationship between the AVP and his or her teams. Begin by directly asking the VPSA these types of questions, speaking to colleagues who have worked with the VPSA before, and reaching out to people who know the VPSA.

Communicate and Filter

The AVP serves a dual role as leader and as someone who supports the long-range vision of the VPSA and the university. In a supervisory and management capacity, the AVP connects actions to mission and vision, but doing this effectively while managing external relationships on campus requires a significant amount of filtering and communicating. Peggy Burke, associate vice president for student development at DePaul University, phrased it this way:

> As an AVP, I have to remember I'm not the supervisor of a smaller student affairs division. Since the role is in the middle between the vice president and the director, the AVP must bridge the gap. Supervising the director is holding the director accountable to the division's goals. Reporting to the vice president is synthesizing what I have heard from my directors back to the vice president.

Dan Maxwell, associate vice chancellor for student affairs for the University of Houston System, and associate vice president for student affairs at the main campus, offered:

> Managing up is how you work with the VPSA. The flow of information is crucial between the VPSA, you, and the directors. The ability to resolve issues before they are a crisis is critical, and to effectively serve as a liaison—officially or unofficially—with campus partners is a must.

Both of these perspectives demonstrate how important it is to navigate the "space between" the VPSA and the director team and how information is shared between these two entities as well.

Furthermore, AVPs have access to sensitive information, as well as some half-formed ideas from the senior management and leadership of the campus. If any of this information were to be shared more broadly, the institution could face legal ramifications or receive negative press. AVPs have to become masters at filtering information for their teams so that information flows freely while incomplete or sensitive information is shared only at the right time and in the right way. Hernandez put it this way, "In the AVP position, you are privy to an enormous amount of information—some that cannot be shared, some that can be helpful or damaging if not delivered in a prudent manner." Developing sound judgment about when to share specific information and with whom is a critical skill for an AVP's success.

Create Positive Working Relationships with Your Staff

Concurrently with the aforementioned focus areas, AVPs need to understand how to actively supervise director-level leaders within their portfolio of responsibility. Most AVPs have already learned the basics of supervision during their careers prior to this role. However, the tenets of supervision are applied to director-level staff differently. Burke explained, "The AVP needs to recognize this is a different role. They cannot go in and be just a 'super director.' A director needs a certain level of respect, responsibility, and expectations." Creating clear expectations, understanding the team's strengths, understanding the strengths and career aspirations of each member on the team, understanding the functional areas under the AVP's oversight, developing an awareness of the diverse needs of team members, and ensuring individual accountability and recognition are all components of creating positive working relationships with your direct reports.

Develop Clear Expectations

Supervisors have a responsibility to those they supervise to spell out their expectations regarding duties, goals, and behaviors. AVPs have this same responsibility to their teams. AVPs must know themselves and their supervisory approach well enough to explain these to their team members. These expectations act as a road map for building and sustaining a solid and positive relationship between supervisor and supervisee. Norb Dunkel, associate vice chancellor for student affairs at the University of Florida, advised, "Provide directors information on what the expectations are for reporting to you (i.e., professionalism, meetings, schedules, organization, communication, etc.)—I have a list of 12 expectations for reporting to me that I review with directors on an annual basis."

To develop these expectations, start with the job description for each person you supervise, and talk with each individual about what he or she needs from you as a supervisor. As this relationship evolves, the AVP and supervisee should review the expectations several times; the AVP must remain open to an evolving conversation in order to maintain a positive connection with staff. Professional competencies associated with the director's specific functional area of responsibility are another resource for the AVP.

This conversation is the beginning of developing trust between the AVP and directors. Both sides should focus on a positive, mutually beneficial outcome as expectations are developed, shared, and refined. Additionally, once these expectations are set, it is crucial for the AVP and the director to meet these expectations and to hold each other accountable.

Understand the Power of the AVP Position

Power affiliated with an AVP position is different from that for a director. When an AVP points out a process flaw, a facility challenge, or a policy need, oftentimes the observation can be mistaken for a directive. French and Raven (1959) introduced a framework for understanding power that includes five distinct bases: coercive power, expert power, reward power, referent power, and legitimate power.

Coercive power involves influence of the supervisor, and it has the potential to cause a negative association for a noncompliant subordinate (or supervisee). Expert power manifests itself in information, knowledge, and wisdom; in good decision making; in sound judgment; and in accurate perception of reality. Reward power is derived from the ability to facilitate the attainment of desired outcomes by others. Though it is closely related to coercive power, the former is conducted from a more positive frame. Referent power is connected to affiliations individuals make with groups or organizations. Legitimate power comes from the formal responsibilities and authority granted to the AVP position.

Raven (1965) later added a sixth base of power—informational power—which involves an individual using information to influence a situation or another individual, either in a positive or negative manner. In subsequent research by Raven (1992) and by Lee and Low (2008), these bases are described not as isolated, but as overlapping and influencing each other.

One AVP recalled an incident in which he made a comment that was seen as a directive:

> I was walking through a building and mentioned that it would be great to get new furniture for a particular location. The associate director of the building was there, and within 3 hours I had furniture pricing e-mailed to me from the director, who also stated in the e-mail, "I didn't realize this was a problem, and am sorry we did not address this." It was an observation, not a directive, and in that moment I was reminded about the power of positional authority.

This example stems from the base of legitimate power and is a cautionary tale for all AVPs. In this situation, the impact of the AVP's statement was not intentional. However, because the AVP was in a position of authority, staff members viewed this statement as the AVP exercising legitimate power and responded accordingly. For the AVP role, understanding these different power bases and knowing when to exercise them in a positive way is important. Of equal importance is to recognize when you may be using these power bases unwisely and to adjust your course of action quickly so that supervisory relationships are not damaged.

Identify Staff Strengths and Career Aspirations

In order to effectively supervise, the AVP needs to understand the strengths of team members and the career aspirations of each. Pendakur explained,

The student affairs axiom of supervising the person still applies to directors, so getting to know who they are, how they work and think, and what their long-term goals are will help you better support each of your directors differently, but effectively.

Strength assessment is crucial in order for the AVP to best guide, coach, and offer opportunities for advancement and development. Both for individual supervisory reasons and for team development, AVPs must understand the gifts, talents, and skills each of the directors brings to the table.

Not all directors have the same long-term career aspirations. Some staff members are ambitious and look to advance their careers, which requires a specific level of development to prepare them for their next step. However, other staff do not wish to advance; rather, they just want to improve within their own field of expertise. Direct reports in this category require a different approach. In order for the AVP to fully understand which approach to take, figuring out what each director needs is critical.

Learn about Functional Areas

The AVP may have more experience than a director in a particular functional area, but for the most part, the AVP is not an expert in all of the areas that make up the portfolio. Tom Ellett, senior associate vice chancellor for student affairs at New York University, stated, "Not having particular 'industry experience' in the area [of your reports] . . . means that gaining industry knowledge is critically important." This area can be one of the most challenging for an AVP, and it was cited by many of the individuals interviewed for this chapter. Hernandez summed up the feeling of many when she said:

> As an AVP, I have moved away from having to be a content expert for all of the departments that report to me. I will never know more about information technology than my director of IT, or about assessment than my director of student life studies.

Nevertheless, the AVP must have some functional understanding of different areas in order to support the director and to advocate appropriately for resources on behalf of that unit. Dunkel explained:

> The biggest challenge I have supervising directors is spending adequate time "getting my arms around" their profession. I have to continuously read, participate, attend events, and the like in the other auxiliary operations to gain a knowledge whereby I am comfortable.

Another strategy used by many AVPs in this type of situation is to ask critical questions of their directors, especially when the AVP is not a content expert. The answers not only provide the AVP with useful information about an operation or a situation, they also provide insight into the approaches, thought processes, and critical thinking skills of staff members. These insights help the AVP understand the needs of staff both operationally and from a personal development perspective.

Empower Direct Reports

When the AVP empowers direct reports, the supervisory role shifts. The AVP no longer directs a team toward a set of goals but acts more like a guide or coach. Banks advised, "Listen to your directors and provide them with the necessary support and resources." Ferguson explained, "I find that this role is more grounded in educating and developing opportunities for directors to better understand best practices and student affairs." Peska acknowledged this shift in his own role as a number two by stating:

> I find that my style of supervision has shifted to more guidance, support, and to address issues once they rise up to actionable offenses. For example, I offer my ear as more of a sounding board to help direct reports understand how their decisions might have broader implications throughout the institution.

Under this supervisory approach, sitting directors lead their own units while still benefiting from supervisory oversight and guidance. Providing a strong outlet for directors to learn about the institution and to understand the "why" behind strategies and priorities creates a successful supervisory relationship at this level.

In order to implement this approach effectively, AVPs need to make themselves available to direct reports in as many ways as possible. Strategies include regular one-on-one meetings (some AVPs reported having these meetings twice per week during peak periods of the year); being available via text and e-mail; and establishing "pop in" hours, whereby direct reports are free to come by the AVP's office knowing the AVP will be there.

Recognize Personal Success

Supervisory relationships at their heart are individual relationships developed between two people, and they involve honesty, communication, and trust. To that end, AVPs need to understand not only the skills and aspirations of their team, but also what is important to them as individuals. This involves more than creating a transactional, professional relationship with staff. It involves moving into the realm of personal success and recognition.

Some directors are quite accomplished in their areas; others want to reach a particular level of mastery. Recognizing when someone has reached a particular achievement is a positive way to reinforce both progress and appropriate behavior. Current AVPs who contributed to this chapter made several remarks about taking a moment to "catch people doing things right" and to reward staff when goals are met. These celebratory moments help create a culture of support and a positive environment in which teams and individuals can thrive.

A powerful way to recognize direct reports, and even other staff within an AVP's oversight, is to nominate staff and projects for institutional, state, regional, national, or international awards; attend celebratory events on campus in which staff are acknowledged; and announce when team members have been recognized.

In addition, some AVPs learn from directors what is happening with second-level staff (those reporting to the director) as well. Peska explained:

> I am more mindful of how far a note of appreciation can go from a second-level supervisor and have asked direct reports to keep me apprised monthly of what is happening in their staff members' lives. . . . It helps when I run into that employee and can offer my condolences or congratulations.

Finally, being present is another way to recognize direct reports and the hard work of their staff. Attending important events, walking around and interacting with staff, and engaging staff in casual conversation allows AVPs to connect more informally with staff and helps staff know that the AVP cares. Dunkel framed it this way:

> Talk to the front-line staff, attend their annual conferences, attend their events, and be seen—your directors and their staff will have a greater respect for you and your work knowing that you care about them and their programs.

Continuing to nurture relationships with staff—both direct reports and beyond—allows the AVP to assist leadership in creating a positive community within the division and at the institution. This in turn provides an empowering environment in which staff members can thrive and the division can reach its goals.

Conclusion

Supervision for an AVP is challenging but also highly rewarding. Developing a solid understanding of yourself and of supervisory expectations from the VPSA; developing clear expectations for the team; and getting to know the talents, strengths, gifts, and aspirations of direct reports help AVPs to develop positive, strong, and empowering relationships with their staff. Being mindful of environment and university priorities also helps directors and their teams accomplish goals that are relevant and in alignment with the direction of the institution and the division. Above all else, creating and maintaining positive supervisory relationships with direct reports help staff and AVPs accomplish both personal and professional goals and, in the end, create highly beneficial experiences for students.

References

American College Personnel Association and National Association of Student Personnel Administrators. (2010). *Professional competency areas for student affairs practitioners.* Retrieved from https://www.naspa.org/images/uploads/main/Professional_Competencies.pdf

Bennett, N., & Miles, S. A. (2006). Second in command: The misunderstood role of the chief operating officer. *Harvard Business Review, 84*(5), 1–8.

Bernard, J. M. (1979). Supervisor training: A discrimination model. *Counselor Education and Supervision, 19*, 60–68.

Bernard, J. M., & Goodyear, R. K. (1998). *Fundamentals of clinical supervision* (2nd ed.). Boston, MA: Allyn & Bacon.

Chagnon, J., & Russell, R. K. (1995). Assessment of supervisee developmental level and supervision environment across supervisor experience. *Journal of Counseling and Development, 73*(5), 553–558.

Covey, S. R. (1989). *The 7 habits of highly effective people: Powerful lessons in personal change.* New York, NY: Free Press.

Dawson, J. B. (1926). The casework supervisor in a family agency. *Family, 6*, 293–295.

Drucker, P. (1988). Management and the world's work. *Harvard Business Review, 66*(5), 65–76.

French, J. R. P., Jr., & Raven, B. H. (1959). The bases of social power. In D. Cartwright (Ed.), *Studies in social power* (pp. 150–167). Ann Arbor, MI: Institute for Social Research.

Hatch, N. W., & Dyer, J. H. (2004). Human capital and learning as a source of sustainable competitive advantage. *Strategic Management Journal, 25*, 1155–1178.

Hawkins, P., & Shohet, R. (2006). *Supervision in the helping professions* (3rd ed.). Berkshire, England: McGraw-Hill.

Herrick, C. D. (1977). *A phenomenological study of supervisees' positive and negative experiences in supervision.* Pittsburgh, PA: University of Pittsburgh Press.

Hock, D. (2005). *One from many: VISA and the rise of chaordic organization.* San Francisco, CA: Berrett-Koehler.

Hodges, T. D., & Clifton, D. O. (2004). Strengths-based development in practice. In P. A. Linley & S. Joseph (Eds.), *Positive psychology in practice* (pp. 256–267). Hoboken, NY: Wiley.

Holloway, E. (1995). *Clinical supervision: A systems approach.* Thousand Oaks, CA: Sage.

Kadushin, A. (1992). *Supervision in social work* (3rd ed.). New York, NY: Columbia University Press.

Kline, N. (1999). *Time to think: Listening to ignite the human mind.* London, England: Cassell Illustrated.

Lee, K. L., & Low, G. T. (2008). Bases of power and subordinates' satisfaction with supervision: The contingent effect of educational orientation. *International Education Studies, 1*(2), 3–13.

Littrell, J. M., Lee-Borden, N., & Lorenz, J. (1979). A developmental framework for counseling supervision. *Counselor Education and Supervision, 19*, 129–136.

Montez, J. M., Wolverton, M., & Gmelch, W. H. (2003). The roles and challenges of deans. *Review of Higher Education, 26*(2), 241–266.

Raven, B. H. (1965). Social influence and power. In I. D. Steiner & M. Fishbein (Eds.), *Current studies in social psychology* (pp. 371–382). New York, NY: Holt, Rinehart and Winston.

Raven, B. H. (1992). A power/interaction model of interpersonal influence: French and Raven 30 years later. *Journal of Social Behavior and Personality, 7*, 217–244.

Salaman, G. (1995). *Managing*. Buckingham, England: Open University Press.
Sandeen, A., & Barr, M. J. (2006). *Critical issues for student affairs: Challenges and opportunities*. San Francisco, CA: Jossey-Bass.
Sanford, N. (1962). *The American college*. New York, NY: Wiley.
Sanford, N. (1966). *Self and society: Social change and individual development*. New York, NY: Atherton.
Squires, D. A. (1978). *A phenomenological study of supervisor's perceptions of a positive supervisory experience* (Unpublished doctoral dissertation). University of Pittsburgh, Pittsburgh, PA.
Stoltenberg, C. (1981). Approaching supervision from a developmental perspective: The counselor complexity model. *Journal of Counseling Psychology, 28*(1), 59–65.
Welch, J. (2005). *Winning*. New York, NY: Harper Collins.
Winston, R. B., & Creamer, D. G. (1997). *Improving staffing affairs practices in student affairs*. San Francisco, CA: Jossey-Bass.
Winston, R. B., & Creamer, D.G. (1999). Staff supervision and professional development: An integrated approach. In W. A. Bryan & R. A. Schwartz (Eds.), *Strategies for staff development: Personal and professional education in the 21st Century* (New Directions for Student Services, No. 84, pp. 29–42). San Francisco, CA: Jossey-Bass.

Managing Fiscal Resources

Sean Stallings, Jason B. Pina, and Amy Hecht

This chapter is an essential part of this book for three reasons. First, we reshape the focus of the associate/assistant vice president (AVP) on budgeting to align with a picture bigger than one department or division. As a senior leader in student affairs, the AVP must not only focus attention on expenditures and division-level revenues, but also know the institutional budgeting processes. Second, AVPs who know their institutions' budgeting process and have a working knowledge of alternative planning approaches become more valuable to the vice president for student affairs (VPSA), especially as institutions move further into times of constrained resources. Third, moving from the concept of budget control to resource management is critical to providing the best outcomes with limited resources for our students. In the American Council on Education series on higher education, Alfred, Shults, Jacquette, and Strickland (2009) described this concept as effectively using all tangible, intangible, and leadership resources effectively.

Beyond the structural management of fiscal resources and understanding the concepts of budgeting, AVPs must harness the opportunity that managing resources at this level presents. Many, but not all, AVPs have the day-to-day responsibility for managing department-level resources. This important leadership distinction separates that type of resource management work and focused time a leader should undertake. This chapter focuses on specific budgeting and resource allocation concepts, but they must be placed within the AVP context. We posit that the AVP has a heightened responsibility to manage resources holistically throughout the fiscal year, not only when an acute issue arises or during "budget time."

Three examples of resource management differences at the AVP level can be taken from the 2015 NASPA AVP Institute. In one session called Strategic Thought and Action, the presenters discussed the importance of vertical and horizontal budget cuts (White & Nayor, 2015). Although comparing and contrasting the relative benefits of across-the-board cuts versus the strategic nature of vertical cuts is not new, the AVP is in the position to work with directors in understanding the intricacies of department-level budgets and in understanding the larger divisional directions articulated by the VPSA. An AVP can navigate this landscape only by understanding various budget pressure points and the relative student impact of current resource allocations.

The second difference of AVP leadership in resource allocation and management is the role of intangible resources. Although an AVP's understanding of higher education budgeting, internal processes, and department-level pressure points is important, it is an incomplete picture of resource management. The AVP is uniquely positioned to assess the internal and external cultures related to budgeting. The division's (or specific department's) reputation for managing resources is an important indicator of whether it is an effective steward of resources. Like much of the AVP's work, relationships and interpersonal interactions have a great impact on resource management. On many campuses and within many student affairs divisions, the importance of the work and the cost–benefit analysis of student outcomes is not well understood or articulated. This common disconnect increases the vulnerability of student affairs resources. AVPs have the opportunity to not only manage resources but also educate key colleagues across campus on the impact these resources have on the student experience.

The third difference between department-level resource management and the AVP role concerns the future. Collaborating with the VPSA, the AVP must articulate upward the current and near-future needs of departments while simultaneously translating the VPSA's vision and divisional direction downward to departments. This fine balance is a key part of the resource-allocation process and factors deeply into change management. The challenges of student affairs work never cease, and it is critical that AVPs lead the discussion on resource management as a tool to improve student success and help the division fulfill its vision.

This chapter is divided into two sections. The first provides a context for understanding the portfolio, division, and institutional budgeting process. The second section speaks to the AVP's responsibility to understand the larger institutional concept. For that we ask the AVP to take the perspective of a CEO of an organization. This important shift in perspective highlights the AVP role relative to other student affairs positions. A leader must understand not only program or initiative concepts but also the relative impact of the resources utilized. Although no single finance-related chapter can cover the complexity of higher education finance, we hope to shift the perspective of the AVP's role in effective resource management.

Portfolio, Division, and Institutional Budget Process

Without question, a chief priority of any new AVP is to understand the multiple complexities that shape the budget of the institution. Brinckerhoff (2000) suggested that "managers need to know where the money comes from, where it goes, what causes income and expenses to go up or down, and in general to understand the finances of the organization" (p. 177). This does not mean that you need to run out and get an MBA, but it does emphasize the importance of having an elevated view of the organization. Surely, you need to understand the scope of your own portfolio, but a divisional leader is simultaneously cultivating an operational understanding of the scope of the division *and* the institution. This understanding begins with an environmental scan that identifies the funding sources for the division, the institutional budget process, and the fiduciary responsibilities and stewardship while providing a roadmap for developing a plan.

The environmental scan provides a context in which the AVP operates by identifying the uncontrolled and controlled variables that have an impact on the present state. It examines the internal factors as well as external factors, but it is not a strengths, weaknesses, opportunities, threats (SWOT) analysis. Rather, an environmental scan provides important information that helps drive the development of a SWOT analysis. Identifying financial opportunities without a clear understanding of the rules and regulations about financial management and revenue generation within the institution can prove problematic. Bryson (2010) recommended identifying the political, economic, social, and technological forces during the environmental scan, because these compel organizations to respond.

Upon completion of an environmental scan, begin to develop a SWOT analysis, which might provide a strategic focus for the next year or more, depending on the institutional or divisional financial picture. For illustrative purposes, a SWOT analysis on the housing unit might reveal the internal strengths to be strong reserves, relatively young mechanical systems, and a very good furniture replacement plan. Internal weaknesses of that same unit might be the growing infrastructure needs for student- and administrative-use technology. External opportunities might be identified as the potential to grow conference programs, an expiring contracted service that can yield a capital contribution in the next bid process, and academic partnerships. External threats may be the nearby construction of a new housing development targeting students.

With an environmental scan and subsequent SWOT analysis, the AVP can explore a strategy that mitigates the threats and maximizes the opportunities. For instance, if a new housing development competes for the college's students, the focus of investment may be to elevate the priority of developing partnerships that enhance the quality of campus living and provide a quality that cannot be replicated in an off-campus location. Another priority shift might be the consideration given to advancing the technology infrastructure in the residence halls to offer services or programs that cannot be duplicated or cannot capitalize on the economies of scale that a campus housing program can.

Funding Sources and Management

Concerning the portfolio and the division, various funding sources have been clouded as "college" money. Although it is indeed all college money, funding sources generally dictate allocation and spending patterns; therefore, you need to have a good handle on the sources feeding the division and the parameters around managing those resources. There are a multitude of higher education funding sources beginning with tuition, government appropriations, student fees and fee-for-service revenue, fundraising, and revenue generated from auxiliary services.

Tuition

Undergraduate tuition is the engine that drives much of higher education in the private sector, and it is becoming more important in the public sector (Barr, 2002). In 2009, tuition and fees represented approximately 26% of total revenue for private institutions, while tuition and fees represented approximately 17% of total revenue for public institutions (National Center for Educational Statistics, 2009). The connection of tuition to a revenue that represents a fifth to a quarter of total income illuminates the importance of enrollment management, because many budgets are built off assumptions of the next year's enrollment. Specifically, student affairs units are typically funded by enrollment and general (state appropriations) revenue dollars, sometimes referred to as E&G. If the student affairs division fails to understand the importance of enrollment management, the division itself could face devastating consequences; with limited funds from the aforementioned pool, student affairs units find themselves competing with the academic core for limited resources.

Government Appropriations

Often a formula-based budget made at the state level, government appropriations go into the same pool to make up the E&G budget and are distributed to advance the college's programs and services. Federal support is received in the manner of grants and loans, while state aid for qualifying institutions is received in appropriations. Even among private institutions, there can be some state support, such as funding for education opportunity programs. Despite declining support from the state, accountability is rising, and budget managers must understand what money is coming in and appreciate the responsibilities associated with managing the funds.

Fees

Student fees are additional charges to students on a term basis. The fee, by design, is earmarked for specific purposes and intended to avoid confusion with tuition dollars. Student fees can range from building fees and activity fees to technology or service fees. Private institutions are much less likely to adopt the strategy of mandatory fees as a means to generate income. Many of the programs and services at public institutions that are supported by such general student fees are funded from tuition income in private institutions (Barr, 2002). Often, with a higher tuition rate, charging additional mandatory fees proves detrimental to the relationship with students. If a private institution elects to charge additional fees that are feeding the student affairs budget, that spending needs to be purposeful and strategic with those particular resources.

Whatever fee revenue is feeding the account, it becomes an AVP's fiduciary responsibility to ensure that the fees remain appropriate and distinct for their purpose. Student activity fees should remain aligned with activities that are tied to the overall student-life experience, while service fees are to remain specific to a service. Temporary or one-time fees naturally are to be used for the one-time purpose of its adoption. To ensure a balance of funds that meet these criteria, you should work with department heads in a careful review of the budgets (income and expenses) to determine whether the income is associated with a specific activity or service. When funds are associated with a specific activity or service, there should be evidence that the funds are used for that purpose. Begin by using a simple pro forma for that unit and see whether the fees collected are truly covering the expenses generated. Should the analysis prove out of balance, this is a red flag that the unit or its work (or both) is being subsidized by another source. Identify which expenses are exceeding the fee rate and perhaps develop justification for a fee increase or reallocate, because in the end, students trust that the fees charged are justified.

Fundraising

The need for justification is never more evident than in the realm of fundraising. Some student affairs units have their own development function, while others benefit from the services from a centralized development office. Apart from the structure, the principles remain the same: Funds generated by donors may be earmarked for specific purposes, particularly if the funds show up in the student affairs budget for programs such as leadership development or peer mentoring. Donor giving that is not earmarked for specific needs is usually allocated to the general fund. Therefore, when managing an account that receives donor funds, determine whether the donor had an intended purpose. As the financial steward, ensure that the funds are aligned with that giving interest and not reallocated to meet another administrative need.

Auxiliary Units

Comparably, revenue generated from auxiliary units should also primarily support the auxiliary function. However, an auxiliary unit can share resources. In that case, the AVP needs to examine the financial health of the auxiliary unit(s). The charge of an auxiliary unit is to be a self-sufficient enterprise, and beyond that purpose it can also serve as a means for the broader division and institution to achieve its mission. As an example, with a healthy auxiliary unit that is thoughtful about reserve budgeting, capital planning, and debt service, the AVP can use its revenue to provide seed money for the VPSA's new initiative. In other cases, the auxiliary unit can assume partial financial responsibility, provided that the program benefits the students generating the revenue. For instance, it is reasonable to use revenue generated from housing to help offset the costs of a campus shuttle on a residential campus that does not permit first- and second-year students to have cars. The residential students realize a significant benefit from the service and would likely be the primary users.

AVPs inevitably find themselves with fiduciary responsibility for one or the entire sources of funds mentioned here. The primary objective should be to conduct an environmental scan identifying the funding sources within the unit of responsibility and the division. In doing so, find where opportunities can be leveraged and threats minimized.

Budget Models

Building on the AVP's theoretical and practical knowledge of financial management in higher education, this section brings various pieces of knowledge together. Barr (2002) and Mian (2013) highlighted several budget models worth noting, including zero-based budgets, incremental budgeting, formula-based budgeting, and responsibility-centered management. AVPs need to know which model or hybrid is used by their institution.

Zero-based Budgeting

Self-explanatory in description, zero-based budgeting assumes that all budgets revert to zero for the upcoming budget-planning year. Respective units are expected to provide justification for all requested dollars in the upcoming year. Such a process could prove helpful to new AVPs, because it provides insight into how the units within the portfolio are using—and justifying the use of—resources. Such a careful review of the budget annually provides a platform for ensuring resources with the division align with the institution's goals and minimizes the likelihood of continuously funding initiatives that no longer resonate with the institution.

Incremental budgeting

The principle of increasing the budget incrementally across the board is a practical and arguably efficient budget model, because inherent increases that address the cost of doing business—such as pay increases based on union contracts—are built into the budget. Using incremental budgeting, managers can quickly calculate expected increases in the new fiscal year. Unfortunately, incremental budgeting fails to offer the same kind of scrutiny as zero-based budgeting and can create blind spots for the AVP in terms of where money can be saved or reallocated. Careful consideration should be given to adopting this method when you are unaware of all the expenses within the AVP's purview, particularly when joining a new institution.

Formula-based Budgeting

Oftentimes, states use formula-based budgeting when determining appropriations for state-supported institutions of higher education, which tie the funding to enrollment (Barr, 2002). If an institution receives state funds based on a formula model, the astute AVP realizes the importance of enrollment management and the role student affairs plays in keeping the institution solvent. The formula model at the state level may assert that each full-time student is worth X dollars while part-time students have a lower value as it relates to appropriations. Used at the institutional level, unit allocations based on formulas may assert that program participation, members on a team, or students in a particular major yield higher allocations.

When the AVP's areas of responsibility are the direct beneficiary, formula-based budgeting can prove fruitful. In contrast, when the areas of responsibility are negatively affected by the formula, the shortfalls of this model become readily apparent. The effects indicate whether to keep the division in favor or identify a way to ensure that the division earns its recognition in order to benefit from the formula used.

Responsibility-centered Management

Responsibility-centered budget models attempt to hold the unit accountable for managing resources. The unit assumes responsibility for balancing the budget and evading deficits. This budget model provides an incentive to the management process, because budget managers who are good stewards of their financial resources can carry forward dollars to be used for more costly goals. The method challenges budget managers to remain attentive to the revenue and expenses far more closely than any of the previously mentioned methods.

The responsibility model is often seen among auxiliary units such as housing. In housing programs where the unit must be self-sufficient, the housing director sets rates and manages occupancy and expenses. When influencing decisions on capital investments and managing the enterprise effectively, the director understands that good stewardship of the resources results in savings that can be reinvested into the program. Other units within the academy are slowly advocating for responsibility or being encouraged to assume responsibility. The responsibility-centered model cultivates and rewards the entrepreneurial spirit within the division.

Nevertheless, the AVP should be wary about jumping on the bandwagon for responsibility-centered budget models before recognizing the full financial picture. As stated, a balanced budget depends on the financial stewardship of the unit managers. However, the unit managers are not always in control of the costs. For example, operating under this model, student health services may be responsible for managing inventory such as vaccines, yet student health services does not control the volume of students that may use the inventory in a given year. In other words, outside forces are at work that have a direct impact on various units. The shrewd

AVP maintains a perspective on how the systems are connected. Without proper planning, an increase in enrollment can radically affect the costs of another unit.

No budget model is perfect, but the AVP must understand the budget model used by the institution, the timeline associated with budgeting, and the opportunities available in any given model.

Budget Development Cycle

Regardless of which budget model has been inherited, the AVP is expected to see 5 years into the future (which is always a little cloudy), as well as the upcoming year. The process is typically driven by the college's chief financial officer (CFO), and at state-supported institutions in many instances it is responsive to the governor's budget. The process looks something like this:

- The CFO consults with fellow cabinet officers and the president about the projected budget and develops a set of priorities and guidelines that influence the budget-development process along with the expected timeline.
- The CFO issues a communication to budget managers regarding the timeline and guidelines as well as any instructions for utilizing budget-modeling software.
- The VPSA communicates an internal review process for budgets prior to final submission.
- Budget leads, such as the AVP, create processes in which multiple levels across the units can communicate unit-related priorities, needs, and investments.
- The AVP needs to consult with the VPSA and advance recommendations. This is part of the vetting process; the AVP should not communicate all wants and desires when advancing recommendations.

- Some processes allow for scenario planning, which might ask budget managers to consider the budget implications of a 10% cut or a 10% increase or a shift in enrollment or service demand.
- The AVP reviews the budget within the context of multiple units and additional recommendations for increase or reductions.
- The budget is submitted to the VPSA for final approval.

Submitting a budget approved by student affairs does not mean the process concludes. To the contrary, now equipped with all of the budgetary requests from the campus, the CFO and the cabinet continue their work, likely for months, to provide a finalized budget for the president.

Throughout the process, opportunities for consultation with those closest to the work should be incorporated, within reason. Incorporation of multiple levels into the process minimizes blind spots, provides for excellent professional development opportunities, and removes the mystery of how budgets are made.

Additionally, Mian (2013) offered an excellent and far more comprehensive budget development timeline used in most colleges and universities. This resource should be considered when seeking budget timeline models for adaptation or for a better understanding.

Business Analysis: Cultivating Your Inner CEO

Executive leadership in higher education necessitates the ability to think more broadly than ever before. As an institutional leader, the AVP is no longer responsible for an individual unit. Divisional leadership must operate with a passion for the success of the institution as a whole. As such, AVP's management and counsel must consider the broader issues facing the division and manage limited resources with precision. Clarke (2002) urged that budgeting and financial reporting should be structured so that the institution's goals are advanced, rather than those of any individual unit. To achieve this end, AVPs need to look at the institution through the lens of a business executive. Financial responsibility compels them to watch for emerging opportunities that advance the college's mission or cause mission creep. Conversely, all opportunities may not prove viable options without systems thinking and a view from a higher plane.

Assuming an institution perspective, the AVP is presented with ideas for advancing new initiatives within the division or provides insight on ideas facing the campus. In each instance, the AVP should exercise a proven method of decision analysis and remain as objective as possible. To help with objectivity, consider the full picture when evaluating proposals (particularly new ones). Units within the academy are systematically connected; shifts in one aspect of the institution can create ripple effects across other units. For example, an institution looking to expand program offerings in academic affairs that would add an additional 100 students must consider how the expansion affects such areas as dining centers, fitness centers, counseling services, tutoring, and so on. Sometimes the needs of the population require increased time on task for the staff, or the timing of the program may not effectively factor in building the turnover time needed to be sure the institution is capable of providing premiere service. Oversight of the ripple effect in decision making can have huge impacts on the financial strength of any existing or new initiative.

Operating as an AVP, keep the ripple effect in mind and incorporate it into the mental processing when reviewing costly initiatives. Suppose the VPSA or chancellor has just returned from a cabinet meeting and has informed the AVP that the institution is advancing an initiative to introduce a new program that will bring approximately 88 international students to study on campus for the winter break. The targeted program fee is $795 per student. The provost has already begun the work of securing faculty to teach the class and has looked to the VPSA for assistance to develop the student life components of the program. The AVP has been charged with working with the division to figure out the implications for this program and to determine whether it is priced right to generate net revenue gains. What should the AVP use to inform the analysis?

Decisions should not be based solely on the premise that the program sounds good. A program that sounds good can create mountains of work and result in unintended financial consequences down the line if it is not properly vetted. Sound decision making can be helped by complex financial analysis, but for the sake of simplicity try starting with a simple pro forma. A pro forma is a financial statement providing a broader financial picture of the profits over losses often used before making an investment (see Table 7.1). Develop a pro forma with contributions and input from colleagues across campus who may be better positioned to assess the real costs associated with an initiative that will depend on their services.

Table 7.1. Pro Forma for a New Initiative

Costs	Year 1	Year 2	Year 3	Year 4	Year 5	Total
Program projected revenue	$70,000	$70,000	$70,000	$70,000	$70,000	$350,000
Program startup costs and faculty	($20,000)	($5,000)	($5,000)	($5,000)	($5,000)	($40,000)
Project personnel	($15,000)	($15,000)	($15,000)	($15,000)	($15,000)	($75,000)
Housing costs	($14,000)	($14,280)	($14,565)	($14,856)	($15,154)	($72,855)
Housekeeping	($2,800)	($2,800)	($2,800)	($2,800)	($2,800)	($14,000)
Health services	($3,500)	($3,500)	($3,500)	($3,500)	($3,500)	($17,500)
Tutoring center	($1,250)	($1,350)	($1,450)	($1,550)	($1,650)	($7,250)
Public safety	($4,800)	($4,800)	($4,800)	($4,800)	($4,800)	($24,000)
Energy costs	($1,000)	($1,200)	($1,400)	($1,500)	($1,500)	($6,600)
Real costs	($62,350)	($47,930)	($48,515)	($49,006)	($49,404)	($257,205)
Net revenue	$7,650	$22,070	$21,485	$20,994	$20,596	$92,795

As presented, the 88 participants charged at a rate of $795 each were projected to yield $70,000 in the first year and $350,000 within 5 years. On the surface, this is an easy program to get behind and support. However, a simple pro forma identifies the real costs and a more accurate picture of the net revenue (the pro forma can have as many rows of costs as necessary). After accounting for projected expenses, the AVP sees that the net revenue yields only $7,650 in first year and only $92,795 within 5 years, still a positive gain but significantly different from the projected $350,000 figure. According to Brinckerhoff (2000), a key element to financial empowerment is an awareness of what you earn and what you lose. In this scenario, your evaluation needs to answer this question: Does it make sense to invest $257,205 during 5 years to make $92,795, or can that investment yield a better return on other initiatives?

Conclusion

Budgeting, like many other competencies within the AVP position, takes on a new perspective and builds on former skills. Although budgeting may be a skill that many AVPs have already mastered, this shift in perspective requires an expanded skill set to help the division and the VPSA be successful. In summary, AVPs should keep the following in mind:

- The first priority for new AVPs should be to understand the finances, where funds come from, and how they are used. An AVP should quickly gain an understanding of the institution's financial processes and funding sources.
- AVPs should shift their perspective on finances from departmental to their portfolio and the broader division.
- AVPs must find a balance between day-to-day financial operations and partnering with the VPSA to develop more long-term funding strategies that align with priorities.

- AVPs should be adept at conducting cost–benefit analysis and understanding the financial impact of decisions.
- AVPs should find creative ways to articulate the impact that resources have on the student experience. This allows them to effectively advocate for resources and assist in maintaining accountability.

References

Alfred, R., Shults, C., Jacquette, O., & Strickland, S. (2009.) *Community colleges on the horizon: Challenge, choice or abundance.* Lanham, MD: Rowman & Littlefield.

Barr, M. (2002). *Jossey-Bass academic administrator's guide to budgets and financial management.* San Francisco, CA: Jossey-Bass.

Brinckerhoff, P. (2000). *Mission-based management: Leading your not-for-profit in the 21st century* (2nd ed.). New York, NY: Wiley.

Bryson, J. (2010). Strategic planning and strategy change cycle. In D. Renz (Ed.), *The Jossey-Bass handbook of non-profit leadership and management* (3rd ed., pp. 230–261). San Francisco, CA: Jossey-Bass.

Clarke, S. (2002). Supportive financial systems. In R. Diamond (Ed.), *Field guide to academic leadership* (pp. 295–310). San Francisco, CA: Jossey-Bass.

Mian, A. (2013). Budgets and reports. In N. Dunkel & J. Baumann (Eds.), *Campus housing management* (Vol. 4, pp. 14–37). Columbus, OH: Association of College & University Housing Officers–International.

National Center for Educational Statistics. (2009). Revenues of Title IV institutions, by level and control of institution, accounting standards utilized, and source of funds: United States, fiscal year 2007 [Data file]. Retrieved from http://nces.ed.gov/datalab/tableslibrary/viewtable.aspx?tableid=4632

White, L., & Nayor, G. (2015, January). *Strategic thought and action.* PowerPoint presentation at the National Association of College Personnel Administrator's AVP Institute, Long Beach, CA.

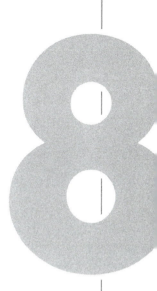

Beyond Balance
Developing Work-Life Integration

Jason B. Pina

"Work to live, not live to work." This ubiquitous prescription is difficult to follow. "A 2008 Harvard Business School survey of 1,000 professionals found 94% of people worked 50 hours or more a week, and almost half worked in excess of 65 hours a week" (Douglas, 2014, para. 15). These data illustrate a perceived lack of balance in life. Although this chapter discusses some historical markers that further endorse this monolithic view of work–life balance (e.g., hours worked), such markers are further evidence of how dated the concept of work–life balance has become. The title of this chapter signifies the importance of accepting that lives are too complex to balance.

We outline strategies in this chapter to further a professional's work to integrate various aspects of life.

The associate/assistant vice president (AVP) position is unique in its scope and role within and across institutions of higher education. This chapter is designed to give AVPs tools to harness professional opportunities while guiding them to integrate four distinct aspects of life—work, home, community, and the private self (Friedman, 2014). Popularized within the term *work–life integration*, this approach recognizes the reality of many AVPs and offers a nuanced strategy to take advantage of the unique benefits that lay within your whole life.

Although work has always been a critical part of human life, the concept of work–life balance is relatively new. As technology advanced and more women entered the workforce in the 19th century, men began to spend more time at home. The U.S. government initially took an active role in limiting formal work hours as a means to increase safety as well as to reduce children in the workplace. Government intervention continued to reduce the number of hours individuals spent at work through retirement benefits, disability assistance, compulsory education, subsidies for the poor and unemployed, and child-labor laws (Levitan & Gallo, 1990).

As legislation reduced the time individuals spent at work, specialization in higher education developed along a parallel path. Faculty who typically ran the institution in and out of the class began to specialize in academic and administrative pursuits. The pool of nonacademic employees that fulfilled duties once undertaken by professors morphed into the field of student affairs. Residential colleges and "house systems" at the turn of the century exploded into full-fledged student affairs divisions in the 20th century. The Morrill Act and GI Bill ushered in the growth of higher education enrollment and student demands for more support and services.

This chapter is a response to the history of work and student affairs at a senior level. Our professoriate colleagues—through the act of specialization and collectively bargained staff—have raised the issue of work–life balance for decades. Oftentimes, this discourse has centered on the rights of women in the workplace (e.g., maternity leave), age- and disability-related protections, and compensation issues. Although this chapter outlines a number of issues regarding work–life balance, it offers an approach to what Friedman (2014) referred to as *integrating* work and life.

Although the concept of balancing work and life is timeless, the American Association of University Professors (2001) outlined a number of important issues. From alternative work schedules, on-campus childcare centers, and elder-care services, the drive to support faculty development and retention in the workforce has improved work–life balance for many. Very few student affairs positions are confined to traditional hours and work weeks. These campus policy changes, coupled with the enactment of a number of laws, allow individuals to embark on successful career paths and participate in how the academy supports employees.

How an individual lives his or her life is as unique as a fingerprint. This chapter is not a prescription for maximizing your potential but serves as a resource to reassess your approach. This chapter examines time management and prioritization as key foundational pieces to integrating aspects of the AVP's life; posits guidance questions to promote the self-examination of many core beliefs that drive important decisions AVPs make daily; and concludes with the importance of assessing your life path and developing resiliency.

Uniqueness of the AVP role

The AVP role is unique and diverse in its description. Although few AVP roles are designed the same, three shared dichotomies shape the role's uniqueness. The students-versus-administration aspect is as unique as the types of AVP positions. In many cases, the AVP does not serve as the main point of contact and may be perceived as always siding with the administration. The second polarity is the division versus the institution. As a key support of the vice president for student affairs (VPSA) and division representative throughout the institution, the time in the AVP role serves as a transitional one. The final conflict that may be the most obvious but is often difficult to navigate is that between the VPSA and departmental leadership. Serving as a conduit between these two entities is the main rationale for the AVP at many institutions. Executing the strategic initiatives of the VPSA while supporting the day-to-day activities of departments within the AVP portfolio adds a significant level of complexity and pressure to the role.

Although not universally true, the AVP and VPSA roles are seen as largely devoid of student interaction. The irony is almost laughable: As your career is recognized and rewarded through promotion, a key job satisfaction component—student interaction—drops precipitously. Outside of large and complex departmental directorships, this transition largely begins to occur at the AVP level. Student affairs professionals often find a counterbalance to the administrative responsibilities through student interaction. AVP role definition and demands may add to your inability to find work–life integration.

Time Management

As many have found, work–life balance is impossible to perfect long term. As Friedman (2014) stated, "The idea that 'work' competes with 'life' ignores that 'life' is actually the intersection and interaction of four major domains: work, home, community, and the private self" (para. 1). A goal of balancing these four domains long term is one fraught with stress and diminished returns. For the AVP, the additional responsibilities make this balance even more complex.

Time management is a key component of any effort to improve your satisfaction with life. According to Vaden (2014), the notion that we can spend equal time in the four domains that comprise life does not seem realistic or worth pursuing. Vaden's (2014) research with more than 2,700 professionals found that successful professionals think differently about time. Building on decades of business-related research and specifically on the popularized work of Stephen Covey (1989, 2005), Vaden (2014) described highly successful professionals as those who "multiply" their time to achieve more success.

Vaden's (2014) time management approach is based on a decision-making model particularly suited for the AVP. The five parts (eliminate, automate, delegate, must be done now, and must be done later) enable the AVP to both organize work and strengthen the division. Improving time management is a key component to achieving work–life integration.

AVPs are bombarded with requests from colleagues across and within their division. In addition, the senior profile also produces additional demands on their time external to the institution. Whether in the community or the larger higher education environment, AVPs are often sought after to continue the work that enabled them to achieve the position and to stretch into unfamiliar environments and activities. The first and most productive time-management technique is to *eliminate*. Requests, routine activities, and cursory invitations grow exponentially as the AVP develops a career and profile. By saying no and being more discerning with time, the AVP can capture more time for the most important and impactful opportunities.

The second tool is used for routine but important activities that cannot be eliminated. *Automating* is defined as the investment of time and resources to ensure the important routine activities are completed without your active time (Vaden, 2014). AVPs should examine responsibilities they are required to undertake but that can be automated.

For example, the documentation of critical and complex enrollment processes throughout one cycle should reduce the planning time during subsequent cycles.

Although eliminating and automating may enormously reduce the AVP's time on many tasks, the third part has numerous direct and indirect benefits: *delegating* tasks and responsibilities to colleagues. The AVP position comes with some latitude on how the portfolio is managed and led. Often, more senior leaders have a "to do it right, I must do it myself" attitude. This approach is often reinforced by their selection as an AVP. Exceptional leaders have proven time after time that their performance exceeds those of their colleagues and warrants recognition and subsequent promotion. To succeed at the next level, the AVP must learn to delegate. The AVP should supervise and mentor when appropriate, but time-management benefits come only from allowing colleagues to have legitimate responsibility to lead efforts and determine outcomes. Eventually, colleagues become more adept in the workplace, begin to have a larger view of the organization, and provide the AVP with critical time for tasks that cannot be eliminated, automated, or delegated.

These tasks are those that the AVPs must and should complete by themselves, either right now or later. After eliminating, automating, or delegating, the AVP can more easily identify those responsibilities that *must be completed now*. You must set aside the appropriate time and devote the necessary concentration to complete those activities. Whether determined by a superior, the cyclical nature of the work, or by an AVP's initiative, some activities are time sensitive, are important, and must not be delegated or automated.

The last group of activities are those that *must be done by the AVP, but not now*. Vaden (2014) said that for this group you are procrastinating on purpose. For many who are driven for success and career advancement, procrastination has a negative connotation. The phrase Vaden used is more a euphemism for patience. AVPs are often faced with long-term opportunities that cannot be resolved in a semester, a year, or even longer. In addition, the complexity of many issues may simply take time to develop, and the AVP may have a specific role that should not be executed in the near term. Senior leaders are often asked to plan strategically, and ultimate success entails higher levels of patience than what was necessary earlier in their careers.

Although generalizable to anyone with a busy life and competing interests, Vaden's (2014) work is specifically useful for the AVP. Unlike previous roles, the AVP role constantly asks the person to make decisions in reaction to immediate needs in order to support the VPSA and the division in the best interests of the institution. The AVP portfolio can dictate to what degree each of these decision points arise and to what extent they conflict, but these decisions are inevitably critical and endless. Because the AVP workload is not finite, time management is an essential skill.

Prioritizing

Although Vaden's (2014) process recoups time lost to unorganized leadership, it falls somewhat short of helping AVPs prioritize the multitude of decisions they face. Andy Stanley often speaks about leadership in the context of church organizations. Two leadership podcasts outlined his *Six Guiding Behaviors and Guiding Questions* that offer guidance in prioritizing for AVPs (Stanley, 2013a; Stanley, 2013b).

Make It better

Many AVPs would not be in the current role if they did not abide by Stanley's (2013a) first behavior, "make it better." The guiding question is: What does the AVP do to help the organization improve? The inquiry is not meant to be a job description outline. The AVP has and will continue to succeed in the areas beyond the job description. This continual improvement drives innovation and enables senior leaders to be more visionary.

Take It Personally

The second behavior is one that is critical in institutional or divisional selection: "take it personally" (Stanley, 2013a). How is the AVP personally engaged in the mission and vision of the institution or division? A rich and nuanced response is the marker of a positive and mutually beneficial relationship. To the degree that the mission and vision resonate with the individual goes a long way to determine performance and role satisfaction. Work–life issues may stem from a mismatch between the AVP and the environment. If this status persists, integration will be hampered by the negativity surrounding the leader's inability to take it personally.

The AVP is uniquely positioned to build relationships throughout the organization. When AVPs collaborate, they leverage for the division the talent and skills of those outside of the department. The ability to break down silos and build relationships increases the opportunities to serve students in a better manner while bringing expertise together.

Replace Yourself

Similar to Vaden's (2014) call to delegate, Stanley (2013b) implored leaders to "replace yourself." As an AVP, replacing yourself is different from empowering colleagues. Succession planning is key to working with colleagues who can take on delegated duties. One consideration in identifying the appropriate individual is his or her knowledge of the larger picture. Surrounding yourself with colleagues who can accept responsibilities usually considered AVP level has significant potential for successful integration.

Stay Fit

The fifth guiding behavior focuses on how to "stay fit" (e.g., spiritually, physically, emotionally, financially, etc.) (Stanley, 2013b). As an AVP, how you take care of yourself is most important for the preservation of self but also is a bellwether of the organization. Given the frontline nature of the AVP, you are observed throughout the organization both personally and professionally. Modeling a "stay fit" attitude represents an important process that introduces work–life integration into the institution. Although the perfection of balance is never achieved during any discernable time horizon, integrating the work of staying fit into the professional setting is an important model for students and colleagues.

Remain Open Handed

AVPs serve at the nexus of new ideas, innovation, and change. Major initiatives that change the division are not always embraced. The final guiding behavior—"remain open handed"—focuses on managing the tension triggered by new efforts that affect individuals and the division (Stanley, 2013b). This tension originates internally and externally. The internal reaction to any new effort to improve the division must be carefully examined. In many cases, apprehension is warranted, and the AVP is uniquely positioned to evaluate the merits of an initiative as it relates to the micro and macro landscapes of the institution. External tension must also be assessed through a thoughtful process. Although a truly unbiased evaluation is difficult to manage (especially when the AVP is the origin of change), it is critical to account for the merits embedded within tension. This process increases the likelihood that the AVP can navigate tension successfully and retain a high level of organizational trust.

Guiding Questions

In this chapter, time management and prioritizing serve as the baseline in determining how AVPs should assess their work–life integration. For work–life integration to be effective, it should be implemented in a dynamic fashion. These components are certainly transferrable to personal lives and oftentimes are inseparable from work-related efforts. The AVP must consider five questions while transitioning to a work–life integration mindset. The responses to these inquiries will shape a personal plan for work–life integration. The groundwork of critiquing current time-management and prioritization practices should be completed prior to responding to these five questions. Similar to what many refer to as a personal mission statement, these questions focus on important roles and aspects of your life and how you want to be when you are at your best.

1. What do you want to mean to others? The first step is to outline the key relationships in your life (e.g., partner, parent, colleagues, etc.). These points of contact span your life and involve individuals and groups in and out of your formal work environment. Using adjectives, list words that describe how you want to be perceived when you are at your best in those relationships. These words should describe you at your best (e.g., I am considerate of other's feelings). You will find the descriptors across many relationships are very similar, if not the same. Responses to this question are an important reminder of your best attributes. A number of tools, such as Gallup's StrengthsFinder can help you identify yourself at your best, but simply reflect on past successes to begin the process. Knowing how you present at your best enables you to have a touchstone when work–life integration is difficult to maintain.

2. Why are you engaged in this work, relationship, or task? Understanding why you are engaged in particular aspects of your life may be cumbersome. This assessment cannot be done in a vacuum or understood through the administration of an instrument. A key statement to help frame the response would be: "I am here to. . . ." Your response can certainly be task oriented, but your statements should include emotional reasons. When work, relationships, or tasks become difficult to navigate, AVPs should be able to return to the roots of why they were originally engaged. Leaders who have prioritized their choices are able to recall compelling rationales for their involvement and to persevere through difficult moments.

3. What can only you do? Whether you are a first-year AVP or a veteran, the role is fraught with the opportunity and desire to work beyond the job scope. This is not an indictment of ambition or stretching the boundary of what have been traditional AVP responsibilities; it is a recognition that a leader's freedom of choice potentially inhibits performance. Goldsmith and Reiter (2007) pointed out that the positive feedback and the successes in a career may lead to increasing responsibility and new roles. They cautioned that small "transactional flaws" prevent some from succeeding at the highest roles in their chosen field (see Chapter 1). Understanding and implementing strategies that help AVPs move toward accomplishing the work only they can do help clarify which actions are best accomplished by others in the organization. Identify those responsibilities and opportunities that only someone at your level can effectively execute and exploit.

4. How can others help you, the division, and the institution? Work life integration should be executed to primarily benefit your role as AVP, which in turn helps you reach your goals throughout your life. Building relationships increases your productivity. Individuals and groups that add value to your role as AVP and the macro work of the institution will in turn pay dividends in professional outcomes and time. Leaders who continually expand and nurture their network more easily find resources that support important work and reduce stress.

5. What role should technology have in your life? The AVP role comes with a number of time-intensive demands. From meetings and committee work to giving speeches or representing the VPSA, the image of passively sitting at a desk and conducting business is not a reality. Appropriately harnessing technology is a key to achieving work–life integration. Many leaders lament the role of technology. The endless e-mails and being available around the clock raise the level of technology-related stress in the working world. Chief executive officer Doug Douglas (2014) stated, "Technology is here to disrupt former modes of 'doing' and revitalize the fractured solutions former professionals thought were most effective." A keystone of this work–life integration model is reframing your thinking of technology to unleash its potential to help you.

Imagine a division of student affairs that has traditional phone lines as the only way to communicate from a distance. This was the reality a generation ago. Whether dealing with a potential crisis, serving on call, or participating in any number of important processes, VPSAs and AVPs were once obliged to remain in their offices or homes to stay available when they could have been doing something else. The limits to what could be effectively managed remotely were great and the impact on personal and family time was enormous.

Fast-forward to contemporary practices that have replaced time-consuming methods that in many cases required leaders to gather in person during off hours. Whether you use video and voice chats with your team, a virtual private network to complete projects, or a cell phone to handle crises, modern technology saves you time. A well-articulated e-mail to several critical parties has replaced numerous phone calls, face-to-face meetings, and traditional memorandums.

Social media has risen to such a level that all AVPs should decide how it adds to their work and fits their personality. Important considerations are the AVP's portfolio, professional involvements, and comfort level with connecting virtually. If social media enhances your professional effectiveness, learn about social media technologies that fit your needs and the institutional culture. Of course, connecting with students virtually and talking with community members through social media is time consuming, but it is practically impossible to replicate this ability within more traditional engagements. The role of technology in your AVP integration plan must match you as an individual, the culture of your institution, and its ability to reduce work-related time.

Bringing It All Together

Leveraging your core personality traits and work-related responsibilities to develop a more integrated life increases the opportunity to achieve desired outcomes. This section highlights two more aspects to work–life integration: your life path and your resiliency. First, to construct a life path, you need to understand how your life to date has influenced your decision-making process and how you currently allocate time to work, home, community, and your private self. Second, because the AVP lifestyle contains both struggle and failure, you need to understand and develop your comprehensive resiliency to those negative episodes.

Constructing a Life Path

Although this book is focused on the AVP role, everyone has unique life experiences and core beliefs defined by much more than a title or a career path. Your personal life path is an amalgamation of the personal and professional choices that have given rise to your current life and summarize the meaning of your life path. The critical step for understanding your life path is to reflect on the internal and external decisions that have shaped work, home, community, and the private self (Friedman, 2014). Bookstores and the Internet are full of resources that guide you through self-discovery. Understanding preferences, vulnerabilities, successes, and failures are incredibly important to making decisions on how to develop work–life integration.

Domains of Resiliency

A successful life is not marked by endless achievements and the absence of failure. To the contrary, preparing for and responding to difficult situations are primary indicators of a life well led. Developing your five resiliency domains—cognitive, spiritual, social, emotional, and physical—leads to work–life integration. Leaders need to develop a sense of consciousness about the level and development of each of these resiliency domains. In practice, the domains take on various forms, depending on your life path and beliefs. Interestingly, real-time benefits will be experienced throughout the development and experiential stages. The power of the domains lies in their ability to bolster your resiliency in difficult times. Well-developed resiliency domains help you lead and deal well with unanticipated outcomes.

Cognitive Domain

The AVP role in higher education straddles concrete and abstract concepts. In a sense, your cognitive development is challenged more by the need to code switch in the role than by the size of the issue. Jean Piaget's (1936) well-known theory of cognitive development highlighted the flexibility needed to successfully navigate complex issues. Withholding judgments when problem solving is a skill that increases your ability to process more complex data in order to make informed decisions. In addition, the AVP's ability to analyze environments and anticipate threats is a powerful tool to help student affairs thrive. The benefits of cognitive development are not confined to work; they appear throughout the work–life integration continuum.

Spiritual Domain

Living by principles of meaning has an important role in developing work–life integration. Many find meaning in a variety of spiritual practices: attending religious services, engaging in healthy practices (e.g., meditation), spending time in nature, and more. Spiritual principles often form the foundation for reacting to serious events in your personal and professional life. Honoring your place on the spectrum of spiritual development allows you to understand the basis of responses to stress. In addition, clarity on your spiritual life may be helpful in any number of personal or professional situations.

Social Domain

Student affairs AVPs are thought to have highly developed social circles, and surely each AVP has social networks and friends. Regardless, critical time should be spent outlining where, how, and why you engage socially. Given the complexity of the role, the AVP should have an increasingly nuanced and supportive social network. Unlike cognitive and spiritual domains, the social domain demands the most external involvement and in some cases requires increased nurturing.

Emotional Domain

Emotional intelligence (EI), a term popularized by Goleman (1985), is a key component of the emotional domain. The better you manage EI in your life by understanding your emotional traits and abilities, the stronger your emotional domain. Along with broader leadership, the AVP position comes with increased scrutiny from others. The way that others perceive you is often influenced by your level of EI. Even though you might have inherited traits that limit your EI development, focused work can raise your awareness of the four EI-related abilities: perceiving, using, understanding, and managing emotion. These abilities are cornerstones to any work–life integration (Mayer, 2002).

Physical Domain

The AVP role, coupled with other life aspects, is inherently stressful. Healthy eating habits, regular exercise, good hygiene, and good sleeping habits are part of a strong physical domain that helps combat stress. Three words are key drivers to improving yourself within this domain: consciousness, primacy, and learning. Many spend significant portions of their lives unaware of physical-related habits that directly inhibit joy. Being conscious of the physical domain helps you address shortcomings and monitor progress. Although few argue that a healthy diet, exercise, hygiene, and sleep do not have positive outcomes on your life, many do not spend the time making the physical domain a priority. Invest the needed time to improve the physical domain. As an AVP, you are embedded in a learning environment; this domain demands a learning mindset. Research related to the physical nature of humans evolves, and that research turns into recommendations, trends, opinions, and new data. The choices you make about your well-being should continuously be assessed and amended when necessary.

Motivational Domain

On its surface, motivation may seem easy to discern and use in our lives, but it may be one of the most underestimated domains of work–life integration. It may be simple to list a number of motivators (e.g., money, prestige, recognition), but to identify their motivation the best leaders look for answers to the question *why*. The answer to the question *why* lies behind both daily decisions and long-term plans; those answers are rooted in your personal values and core beliefs and are the guideposts of motivation. When difficult decisions have to be made or sacrifices endured, an AVP's motivation guides much of the approach and reaction. Sinek (2014) explained how *why* links to a part of the brain that drives behavior and decision making. Knowing *why* increases the chances that you and those around you are motivated to succeed.

Conclusion

This chapter identifies a hierarchical approach to both analyzing current practices and developing a plan that moves away from work–life balance and toward work–life integration. Understanding the external dynamics that influence the AVP role is an important starting point. It helps the leader frame the expectations of work and understand how the roles of home, community, and the private self enter into the integration equation. Although time management may be an age-old issue, it remains a critical core component of an integration plan. The finite nature of time influences every aspect of your personal plan. AVPs should assess their behaviors and determine whether they support or hinder work–life integration. This chapter opened with a timeless saying, "Work to live, not live to work." A personal work–life integration plan allows for growth and success but most important focuses on a well-led life.

References

American Association of University Professors. (2001). Statement of principles on family responsibilities and academic work. Retrieved from http://www.aaup.org/report/statement-principles-family-responsibilities-and-academic-work

Covey, S. R. (1989). *The 7 habits of highly effective people: Powerful lessons in Personal change.* New York, NY: Free Press.

Covey, S. R. (2005). *The 8th habit: From effectiveness to greatness.* New York, NY: Free Press.

Douglas, D. (2014, May 7). Why work-life integration trumps work-life balance [Blog post]. Retrieved from http://www.fastcompany.com/3030120/bottom-line/why-work-life-integration-trumps-work-life-balance

Friedman, S. (October 7, 2014). What successful work and life integration looks like. *Harvard Business Review.* Retrieved from https://hbr.org/2014/10/what-successful-work-and-life-integration-looks-like.html

Goleman, D. (1985). *Emotional intelligence: Why it can matter more than IQ.* New York, NY: Bantam.

Goldsmith, M., & Reiter, M. (2007). *What got you here won't get you there: How successful people become even more successful.* New York, NY: Hyperion.

Levitan, S. A., & Gallo, F. (1990, March). Work and family: The impact of legislation. *Monthly Labor Review, 34*–40. Retrieved from http://www.bls.gov/opub/mlr/1990/03/art5full.pdf

Mayer, J. D. (2002). The effective leader: Understanding and applying emotional intelligence. *Ivey Business Journal*. Retrieved from http://iveybusinessjournal.com/publication/the-effective-leader-understanding-and-applying-emotional-intelligence

Piaget, J. (1936). *Origins of intelligence in the child*. London, England: Routledge & Kegan Paul.

Sinek, S. (2014, March 3). Start with why [Video file]. Retrieved from https://www.youtube.com/watch?v=IPYeCltXpxw

Stanley, A. (2013a, June 7). *Defining your organizational culture—part 1* [Audio podcast]. Retrieved from http://feedproxy.google.com/~r/AndyStanleyLeadershipPodcast/~5/WgL0qzYodow/Defining_Your_Organizational_Culture_Part_1.mp3

Stanley, A. (2013b, July 5). *Defining your organizational culture—part 2* [Audio podcast]. Retrieved from http://feedproxy.google.com/~r/AndyStanleyLeadershipPodcast/~5/n7KpRAJIkDQ/Defining-Your-Organizational-Culture-Part-2.mp3

Vaden, R. (2014). *Procrastinate on purpose: 5 permissions to multiply your time*. New York, NY: Perigee Books.

Maximizing the Role

Cynthia Hernandez

The first years as an associate/assistant vice president (AVP) are an exciting time. Even for those who are promoted to this position from within the organization, everything is new as AVP responsibilities are taken on. Much of the first year is spent learning the organization, understanding the history, learning about the staff, and speaking with internal and external stakeholders to learn the politics and opportunities for the organization. During this time, the AVP also learns how to serve the vice president for student affairs (VPSA), understanding expectations and how to best complement her or him. Days and nights are often busy as a new AVP learns the new landscape and then begins to implement changes that advance the organization. There is never a lack of something to learn and accomplish during the first few years, tending to the urgent and always trying to make room for the important. Time passes quickly and suddenly many AVPs find themselves reflecting on their first 3 years in the position and wondering what the next 3 will hold. AVPs may ask themselves: Do I want to remain in this position? If I do, how can I remain challenged? What can I do to make sure I have the motivation to remain effective in my position? How do I maximize the role?

This chapter includes personal accounts from four current AVPs and one interim VPSA. Each shared what they enjoy about their AVP roles and how he or she continues to be efficient and maximize the role. Collectively they have more than 51 years of AVP experience with tenures ranging from 7 to 14 years. Two have served as interim VPSAs, and only one has definitively expressed a desire to hold a VPSA position. Their AVP experiences have been at large public, large private, midsize public, and small private institutions. In order to provide rich details of their experiences and avoid the perception of the contributors' institutions, identifiable details have been removed from their accounts.

Maintaining Motivated AVPs

Traditionally positioned between the VPSA and director-level reports, the AVP is at the top of the midlevel-administrator hierarchy. The AVP is no longer the "boots on the ground" staff member nor the department head, but the AVP is not quite calling all the shots. However, the AVP position is critical to the success of the student affairs organization. The VPSA leans on the AVP to successfully navigate politics, advance priorities for the division, advocate for students (Coleman, Hecht, Hephner LaBanc, & Michael, 2012), and develop staff. They are asked to "lead from the middle," managing up, down, and across the organization.

As the public cries out for curtailed administrative costs, increased accountability, and fiscal efficiency, VPSAs must show evidence of maximized performance of their human resources. When motivation wanes in any employee, regardless of level, production is affected. Therefore, the concept of maximizing the role and staying motivated has become increasingly important in the current environment. Bardwick (1986) found that an employee reaches a content plateau after achieving expertise in the field or functional area and then becomes bored with work roles. When a mid-level administrator is no longer learning or challenged, he or she becomes a liability to the organization, devoid of ideas, a sense of humor, and an attitude of assistance (Scott, 1975). Understanding what keeps AVPs motivated and effective in their work can provide student affairs leaders with strategies to retain this important population (Hernandez, 2010).

Reasons for Remaining

> When I came to my present institution, I made a commitment to stay for 5 years. In year 2, the vice president decided to create a dean of students office and asked my spouse to be the dean of students. I have been very fortunate throughout my career to have a very supportive spouse who has made personal and career sacrifices to allow me to pursue new opportunities. I was very proud that my wife was named dean of students and wanted to support her in the new role. In year 4, the president decided not to renew the contract of the vice president who hired me. The president appointed a new vice president who asked for my commitment while he was the interim. The interim appointment became a 5-year appointment. I applied for a few VPSA positions of interest during these years. I was offered a VPSA position, but felt the community was not a good place for our family and declined the offer. We have been happy with our personal and work lives in this community. It is a very good place to raise a family. Thus, we did not want to move while our last child was in high school.
>
> —*Interim vice president for student affairs at a large public university*

The reasons for remaining in an AVP position are vast. Career plateauing in an AVP position, either voluntarily or involuntarily, is a reality in student affairs. Midlevel administrators may encounter two types of career plateaus: content and structural. An employee reaches a content plateau when the employee becomes uninterested in the work after reaching a level of real or perceived mastery of the skills and competencies needed. A structural plateau is reached when the employee does not possess the skills or competencies to move up in the hierarchy, there are no open opportunities to move up in the organization, or the employee makes a personal decision to remain at a certain level in the organization (Bardwick, 1986; Appelbaum & Santiago, 1997).

Structural plateaus are categorized as organizational or personal (Appelbaum & Santiago, 1997). An employee reaches an organizational plateau when the employee has the skills, abilities, and desire to advance but is prevented from doing so based on the limited opportunities for advancement. Due to the pyramid-type structure of student affairs organizations, a limited number of VPSA positions exist in the profession, thus limiting the opportunities for AVPs to advance, especially within the same institution. Consequently, many AVPs reach an organizational plateau and remain in the middle of the student affairs hierarchy for the remainder of their careers. To combat structural plateauing, midlevel administrators such as AVPs seek either a horizontal or vertical move to another institution or find ways to be renewed in their current position (Bardwick, 1986; Johnsrud, 1996; Komives, 1992; Sagaria & Johnsrud, 1988).

Alternatively, an employee who does not want to advance to a higher level has chosen a personal plateau (Appelbaum & Santiago, 1997). Some AVPs reach a personal plateau and choose to remain in an AVP position for an extended period of time or for the duration of their career. Collins (2009) studied female midlevel student affairs administrators who turned down opportunities to serve as VPSAs. Through structured interviews with six women in various midlevel positions, Collins found that concerns about time management, increased politics at higher level positions, and the fear of spending even less time with their families contributed to the participants' decisions to remain in their midlevel positions. In addition to the factors identified in this study, many professionals have chosen to remain in their professional role because of the institutional fit.

The role of institutional fit for student affairs professionals has gained increased attention in recent years. Hirt (2006) engaged in a series of comprehensive studies examining how work life varied for student affairs professionals based on the type of institution in which they served, thus exploring the intersection between the work of student affairs professionals and the organizational setting. Ultimately, Hirt found that institutional type affects practice, and, consequently, the institution where midlevel administrators practice may have an impact on their work life. Some AVPs feel called to work at a specific type of institution and place more importance on remaining at that institution than seeking advancement elsewhere.

> With my years of service at the university and the experience I have gained in each aspect of work within the division (having directly supervised almost all areas), I can provide context and a bit of institutional memory. My enthusiasm, however, comes from the opportunities before us. I have a sense that the work I do each day is meaningful. There is a realization that the great accomplishments in my career have come from baby steps taken each day. Few things of value were accomplished or completed overnight. Remembering that encourages me to continue focusing on goals and trying to stay on track each day. The vice president and my other colleagues continue to nurture me, energize me, and help me cast a vision. Beyond that, I, like others with whom I serve, feel called to be at this university. I don't know that I would be as invested in the work I do on another campus. The mission of this university is "to educate men and women for worldwide leadership and service by integrating academic

excellence and Christian commitment within a caring community." Being in a place where I can share my faith is a priority in my life. This university is the place that helped me realize my calling; I want others who come here to know that this is a nurturing environment that will challenge and support them as they develop into contributing citizens of our world. Luke 12:48 inspires me: "Much will be required from everyone to whom much has been given. But even more will be demanded from the one to whom much has been entrusted" (ISV). —*Associate vice president for student life at a large private university*

Similarly, some find the role and responsibilities of the AVP position inspiring. They enjoy the autonomy and flexibility of leading from this upper midlevel position, being able to effect change and make a significant difference but buffered from many of the challenges that face the VPSA. Multiple speaking engagements, extended travel, fundraising, politics, and always being "on" are a few of the reasons the VPSA role is not attractive to some AVPs. These individuals may choose to remain in an AVP role, at their current institution or a different institution, for the rest of their careers.

> Throughout my career, I have worked to position myself to be able to move into an SSAO [senior student affairs officer] role should I choose to do so. I attended the Alice Manicur Symposium sponsored by NASPA a few years ago to hear about the intricacies of the position from women currently serving in the SSAO role. There are many aspects of the SSAO role that are appealing in terms of the ability to set direction at the institution level; however, there are other aspects of the position that I find less appealing. At the SSAO level, particularly at a midsize to larger institution, you are further removed from the day-to-day operations in student affairs. I enjoy the hands-on nature of working with divisional initiatives and providing direct support to staff and departmental operations. My decision to remain in an AVP role was also influenced by a desire to have more balance in my life. As an SSAO, work roles carry over into your personal and community life. As my vice chancellor often states, people

perceive and interact with you in your role as the SSAO no matter the setting. The expectations for being available and participating in campus and community events are much greater at the SSAO level than the AVP level. I enjoy the separation from work and my personal and community life. —*Associate vice chancellor for student affairs at a large public university*

The reasons for remaining in an AVP role for a period of time are varied and personal to each individual. Whether permanent or temporary, it is imperative that AVPs remain motivated and effective in their work in order to best serve the organization.

Remaining Effective

Hughes (2004) contended that "for every student affairs professional who has remained in the same position for 15 years and has continued to learn, grow, and contribute to the field, there is another professional with similar years in the profession who is bored, uninspired, and unhappy" (p. 141). After several years in a position, it is easy to settle into a routine, especially if responsibilities have not changed. It is important to not become so complacent that the work is no longer challenging.

Bardwick (1986) recommended that individuals should seek opportunities to learn and develop professionally to reduce the risk of content plateauing and, consequently, underperforming. AVPs who choose to remain in the position should find ways to continue to be effective in the role. Two strategies have been identified to assist AVPs in remaining effective: (a) remembering the purpose of the work and (b) committing to life-long learning.

Why We Do the Work

As an AVP, the main aspect of the position that I enjoy is that there is never a chance to get bored. No two days are ever alike; just because I have it on my schedule for the day, it may or may not happen today in the way I had anticipated. There are daily opportunities to provide solutions for obstacles students and colleagues face. The AVP role positions me within the organization where I have daily contact with the vice president and frequent interaction with the president and other members of the executive council. I am invited to participate in campuswide initiatives, including the development of policies and procedures. These efforts have broader capacities to influence greater numbers of individuals. Overall, I love my work, the students, and the colleagues I work alongside each day. Nothing in life is more thrilling than working with students from the moment they step onto campus until the time they return, bringing their children to begin their own collegiate experience. Few opportunities exist in life for someone to help shape and influence another's life in such eternal ways. The realization that I have an opportunity to speak into someone's life like that takes my breath away. —*Associate vice president for student life at a large private university*

The role and responsibilities of an AVP vary from campus to campus and can be determined by a myriad of institutional characteristics such as enrollment size, number of staff, and institutional mission. Hemphill (2012) identified critical areas where AVPs should become effective contributors and leaders, especially those interested in ascending to a VPSA position: violence on campus, strategic planning and assessment, cultivating positive student relationships, developing human capital, and navigating institutional culture and politics. AVPs are drawn to the position and remain there because of certain aspects of the work itself. At the core of the work of an AVP is the opportunity to form relationships as well as shape and develop individuals—primarily students and staff.

Impact on Students

Student affairs professionals have indicated the opportunity to affect student learning and development as the main reasons for entering and remaining in the profession. Seeing students grow and succeed is a motivator that drives student affairs professionals to excel in their work and alleviates some of the stressors inherent to midlevel administrators' roles (Hernandez, 2010). In her study of job satisfaction, Bender (2009) found that most student affairs professionals enjoyed working with students and believed the job they do is important. This finding is in keeping with Young's (2001) contention that affecting student learning and development in the context of higher education is a basic tenet of the student affairs philosophy. Student affairs professionals believe in the worth of the individual and hold that "common good can be promoted best by helping each individual to develop to the utmost in accordance with his abilities" (Young, 2001, p. 87). Student affairs administrators believe that their work benefits not only the individual student but also greater society.

> Remember why you chose this profession. The politics will change, leadership will change, students' names and faces will change, but the mission remains the same: Serve our students. —*Assistant vice president for student affairs at a large public university*
>
> I keep myself motivated in my role by recognizing that I am making a difference! I get the opportunity to interact with an amazing group of students who have an amazing gift to give to the world! —*Associate dean of students at a small private college*

Many believe that career advancement results in less direct contact with and a diminished impact on students. The type of interaction with students indeed often changes in an AVP role. At some institutions, the AVP may no longer spend weekend nights in a sleeping bag at a retreat center, but instead drives up for a panel or delivers opening remarks. Often, AVP interactions with students are limited to structured meetings with a focus on getting input on a particular campus issue or policy. Although the interaction has changed, AVPs still find it rewarding to have the opportunity to interact with students on campus and observe these students become successful in their curricular and cocurricular endeavors. Many times an AVP's interactions with students consist of working with students in crisis, in academic or behavior-related trouble, or in circumstances of a grievance. Although finding outcomes to assist students in these situations can be rewarding, these interactions must be balanced with experiences in which the AVP can connect with students under more positive circumstances, such as visiting a student program or organization meeting, enjoying a meal in the dining hall, attending graduation, or speaking at or observing new student orientation. Finding ways to keep connections with students and observe their success are positive reminders of the importance of the work.

> As an AVP, I have the honor to speak to new students and their families at new student orientation. I am energized by their bright eyes and wide smiles as they sit in the audience about to embark on their collegiate experience. I also have the pleasure of seeing them walk across the stage at graduation, the same bright eyes and wide smiles as they embark on a new journey beyond the campus gates. My hope is that they have positive memories of their time here and that we in the division created space for those memories to happen. —*Assistant vice president for student affairs at a large public university*

Supporting and Developing Staff

Hemphill (2012) contended that developing human capital is one of the most important skills that an AVP can acquire in order to build a healthy, successful organization. An AVP must learn to effectively supervise staff and manage human resources with an eye to legal and compliance issues, such as grievances, terminations, and fitness for duty. In spite of all of the complex human resources issues, AVPs identify the recruitment, retention, and development of staff as one of the most rewarding responsibilities in their portfolios. "Managing staff is a critical element of the middle manager's responsibility. Although it is never an easy task, it is frequently the most rewarding" (Mills, 2000, p. 141). Similar to interactions with students, AVPs enjoy the opportunity to help staff grow and develop. They like giving directors autonomy in their areas and often rely on their experiences and expertise in solving complex issues. In order to be successful, an AVP should develop respect and trust with staff. In addition, AVPs must recognize individual differences and identify unique skills, experiences, and interests that enable staff to reach their professional and organizational goals.

> One of the keys to remaining effective in the AVP role is learning not only to delegate but to empower people. Set the vision or give staff the task and let them rise up and shine. Empowering staff can be motivating for them and for me. It allows me to maximize my time and be more productive to focus on the important and balance my schedule. If I have to sit in every meeting and weigh in on every decision then I'm not maximizing my time. In addition, give people the tools to be successful. I learned from a former vice president that "information is power, so share it!" I try to communicate frequently and honestly with my team. The more information people have the better they can do their jobs and provide quality programs and services to students. I believe that good communication quells the proverbial "water cooler talk" that can be toxic to departments or divisions. Also, I try to challenge staff and give them opportunities to be creative and try innovative and new ideas without the fear of failure. Provide chances for staff to work outside of their department and move up or in other positions around the university. Sometimes that means really great staff members move outside the division, but I prefer to have them for a short time doing great work than the alternative. —*Assistant vice president for student affairs at a large public university*

Committing to Life-long Learning

In addition to focusing on the particular aspects of the work that brings enjoyment, AVPs can focus on areas that sharpen skills and enhance competencies in order to remain effective in their role. As the issues in higher education continue to grow in complexity, the AVPs are expected to keep abreast of these issues. With multiple functional areas in their reporting chain, AVPs must be familiar with content-specific information in addition to overarching leadership as well as management, legal, and administrative issues. As the world continues to change so do the issues facing higher education and student affairs; thus, the successful AVP is committed to developing habits and skills that enhance lifelong learning.

Staying Abreast of Higher Education Issues

Staying current on issues facing higher education is critical to the AVP role. In addition to knowing the issues, an AVP must be able to articulate the impact of these issues on their own students, staff, and institution. These changes come swiftly and an AVP must be ready to tackle new things that land on the doorstep. For example, life changed for a number of AVPs when the Office for Civil Rights issued a *Dear Colleague* letter in April 2011 (U.S. Department of Education, 2011). On the heels of the letter came the Violence Against Women Reauthorization Act (2013), amending the Clery Act, which included new processes, training, and education related to sexual assault, domestic violence, dating violence, and stalking. Next, a White House task force released a report ("Not Alone," 2014) with specific guidance for colleges and universities on how to reduce and address incidents of sexual violence. Following federal guidance, many states have also passed their own legislation on how colleges and universities should handle these incidents. Recommendations needed to be interpreted; policies and procedures revised; and training and preventative education programs developed and refined. Other resources and services needed attention, and AVPs found themselves in an oversight role, a deputy coordinator role, or for some in a boots-on-the-ground role.

Keeping on top of compliance and other issues in higher education is important. Absent specific guidelines, AVPs are personally responsible for navigating and keeping abreast of issues that are important to their role. Making time each day to read various higher education news sources and other professional literature, talking with colleagues about issues, and allowing time for personal reflection is important and imperative to remaining effective in the AVP role.

Professional Development Opportunities

Participating in the career-long process of professional improvement, also known as professional development, is an essential component in keeping AVPs effective. Professional development fosters new skills and competencies. A myriad of umbrella and functional-area-specific professional associations offer educational experiences for the student affairs practitioner. Several student affairs professional associations offer publications and educational experiences specific to midlevel administrators. However, little attention has been paid to AVPs as a subset of midlevel administrators and the unique challenges and responsibilities that come with being situated at their place in the student affairs hierarchy.

Until recently, AVPs who wanted to keep their skills and knowledge current have had to read journals selectively, consult with their colleagues, and attend general conferences and workshops that may speak to only portions of their work. Much of the programming for AVPs has been focused on preparing the next generation of VPSAs through aspiring VPSA institutes, workshops, and conference sessions. These efforts, while extremely valuable, may not attract or meet the needs of an AVP seeking to remain in an AVP role.

Since 2012, through the formation of the AVP Initiatives Steering Committee, NASPA has developed a series of preconference workshops, conference educational sessions, publications, and an institute aimed specifically at the role of the AVP. These initiatives provide a community where AVPs can sharpen their practices, enhance competencies, and find sounding boards as they network with fellow AVPs. Although the direct responsibilities of an AVP vary from position to position, there are some overarching competencies that tie these positions together, especially the move from being responsible for department-level issues to division issues. The professional development opportunities geared specifically toward AVPs allow AVPs to approach the conversation on specific topics through their particular lens versus that of a director or other midlevel manager. This approach equips AVPs to excel in their current position and prepares those who are seeking to ascend to the VPSA position.

Maximizing the Role

The traditional pathway to an AVP position usually begins with an entry-level student affairs position, for example, an advising position in student activities, a community director position in residence life, a judicial officer in student conduct, or a programmer in health education. These entry-level roles are usually student focused with little to no supervisory (beyond student staff), budget, or policy development responsibilities. As student affairs professionals move along a career trajectory, they are constantly adding and refining skills relevant to their current, and hopefully next, position. By the time someone reaches the AVP role, he or she has demonstrated an understanding of how to develop skills and competencies that assist in achieving the next level. However, if the motivation for engaging in professional development is to move up in the hierarchy, what happens when someone reaches the goal and loses that particular motivation? Professional development and increased skills do not always result in promotion within the organization, but the positive impact on morale should not be overlooked (Johnsrud, Heck, & Rosser, 2000). Johnsrud (1996) found that midlevel administrators want to improve their skills and acquire new ones. As AVPs strive to make the most of the role, they should seek out and take advantage of the opportunities that arise in the course of the job, build partnerships with colleagues, and find ways to constructively give back to the student affairs profession.

New Initiatives or Areas of Supervision

> I have been fortunate throughout my tenure as an AVP that my role and responsibilities have changed over time even though my title has remained the same. My institution has undergone a major transformation in the last decade so the university feels and looks vastly different from when I started. At times, I don't even recognize this place as the same institution so it doesn't really feel like I've been in the same role for almost a decade. Opportunities to acquire new skills and learn different aspects of student affairs have kept me engaged and excited about my role as an assistant vice president. —*Assistant vice president for student affairs at a large public university*

When an AVP is hired, he or she is usually responsible for overseeing one or more functional areas. As AVPs remain in that role there may be opportunities to expand or exchange functional areas (especially in multiple-AVP structures). In addition to acquiring new reporting units, AVPs can also diversify their portfolios and be rejuvenated by agreeing to take on a new area of focus, such as overseeing division efforts on new compliance mandates (e.g., Title IX, Violence Against Women Reauthorization Act of 2013), accreditation mandates (e.g., quality enhancement plans), enhancing student behavioral intervention, or leading division-focused strategic planning or assessment. With these opportunities, AVPs can sharpen their skills in a particular policy area through education and research, make contact with new staff and university colleagues, and network with AVPs at other institutions engaged in similar work. AVPs should make it known that they are open to receiving new responsibilities or assignments; answering the call when needed can go a long way in building the relationship with a VPSA and remaining invigorated in the position. Rotating reporting areas and taking on new areas of focus are great ways to learn more about the division and remain rejuvenated. In addition, for some AVPs, doing so prepares them to serve as the interim VPSA when called on.

Serving as the Interim

A VPSA departure, either planned or unexpected, can be an anxious time for a division. Will the university leadership reorganize? When will the search begin? Who will be the next VPSA? What do we need to do in the meantime? Often, an AVP is called on to serve as the interim VPSA. The breadth of experiences as an AVP is valuable preparation for an interim role. An opportunity of this magnitude is a big decision and can often confirm an AVP's decision to remain or ascend to a VPSA position. Stepping into the role of the VPSA gives AVPs an opportunity to stretch as they use different skills and competencies to navigate institutional politics from a cabinet level; serve as a voice and chief fundraiser to external constituents; and be the public face of the division to students, faculty, and staff. For some, serving as interim VPSA makes clear that the responsibilities are not congruent with their desires. An AVP who returns to the AVP position returns with a new perspective, relationships with new colleagues, and a new appreciation of and insight into working with the new VPSA. For others, the experience awakens a call to serve in the VPSA position at the same institution, if the opportunity presents itself, or a new institution. Regardless, an interim appointment can be a revitalizing experience for an AVP.

Building Partnerships

> Do your job the best you possibly can. Learn all you can in the role. Seek opportunities to expand the role and become more involved in the leadership of the institution. I believe I have benefited from having diverse experiences. . . . It is crucial to develop positive working relationships with key people at the university and in the community. It is important to be nice to others even when they are not nice to you and do not deserve your attention. —*Interim vice president for student affairs at a large public university*

AVPs should take advantage of opportunities to get involved in larger university discussions that span student affairs and beyond by sitting on or chairing university committees, task forces, search committees, or councils. An appointment to a committee and the work it entails may seem more like an added responsibility than a reward, but this is an opportunity to help the VPSA look his or her best; to reflect well on the division; and to meet, network, and build partnerships with colleagues.

Rosser (2004) determined that midlevel administrators who develop positive relationships with senior administrators, faculty, staff, students, and external constituents tend to have higher levels of satisfaction with their work experiences and are less likely to leave the organization. Ellis and Moon (1991) contended that to survive in the active and fast-paced environment of higher education administration, an administrator must be able to make contacts, link people with ideas, get and give information, and support the projects of others. Building and maintaining positive relationships is an important characteristic of the AVP position. AVPs are in a unique position in the student affairs hierarchy, because they have the opportunity to work and interact with a variety of people. They may have sporadic contact with entry-level staff; frequent contact with directors, other midlevel administrators, and the VPSA; and regular contact with other senior-level administrators beyond the division.

From Involvement to Engagement

Although structural career advancement may no longer be the primary goal for those who remain in the AVP position, they still must enhance their personal and professional development. At some point, midlevel administrators find motivation and fulfillment through giving back to the profession. Komives (1992) suggested opportunities such as writing for scholarly publications, mentoring younger staff, and participating in professional associations as ways to achieve professional renewal and development.

Involvement in professional associations has long been recognized as a way for student affairs professionals to enhance skills and competencies. The seed of getting involved is planted at the graduate and at times even the undergraduate level. Attending conferences, serving as a conference volunteer, and presenting educational sessions are as much rites of passage as they are professional development opportunities for newer professionals. As individuals transition to midlevel positions, a move from involvement to deeper engagement in professional associations begins to occur. Unfortunately, Bryan and Mullendore (1990) found that many midlevel managers use a "shotgun approach" to professional development by engaging in opportunities haphazardly, without an intentional plan.

At the AVP level, involvement and engagement in professional association offerings is key, especially as new reporting areas are added to portfolios and new issues emerge. In addition, many AVPs feel called to give back to the profession, thus the relationship with professional associations turns to engagement. AVPs often are called to serve in key leadership roles in professional associations, they are asked to be mentors, and they are approached for their experience and expertise to serve as editors of journals and produce scholarly work—in essence, lending their voice to the profession. In addition, similar to other involvement opportunities, engagement in the work of a professional association allows AVPs to network with colleagues in similar roles on other campuses. In building a personal and professional network of colleagues, AVPs, especially those within a single-AVP model, learn from the successes and missteps of others and, ultimately, learn to normalize issues.

Conclusion

AVPs are an important part of the student affairs hierarchy. These professionals affect the daily lives of students and contribute significantly to the overall coordination of institutional resources and activities (Hernandez, 2010). In addition, AVPs bring a degree of experience, a wealth of institutional history, and an insight into student affairs organizations that are difficult to replace (Belch & Strange, 1995). Although some seek the VPSA position, for a variety of reasons many remain in the AVP position for an extended period of time or sunset their career in the position. Those who remain risk becoming bored, complacent, and ineffective in their roles, but they can find ways to stay motivated and maximize the role in order to continue serving their organizations.

References

Appelbaum, S., & Santiago, V. (1997). Career development in the plateaued organization. *Career Development International, 2*(1), 11–20.

Bardwick, J. (1986). *Plateauing trap: How to avoid it in your career and your life.* New York, NY: American Management Association.

Belch, H. A., & Strange, C. C. (1995). Views from the bottleneck: Middle managers in student affairs. *NASPA Journal, 32*, 208–222.

Bender, B. E. (2009). Job satisfaction in student affairs. *NASPA Journal, 46*, 553–565.

Bryan, W., & Mullendore, R. (1990). Professional development strategies. In R. B. Young (Ed.), *The invisible leaders: Student affairs mid-managers* (pp. 109–130). Washington, DC: National Association of Student Personnel Administrators.

Coleman, K. W., Hecht, A., Hephner LaBanc, B., & Michael, K. W. (2012). Key competencies for moving into student affairs management: Administrative acumen, leadership capacity required. *Leadership Exchange, 10*(1), 11–12.

Collins, K. (2009). *Those who just said "NO!": Career-life decisions of middle management women in student affairs administration* (Unpublished doctoral dissertation). Bowling Green State University, Bowling Green, OH.

Ellis, H., & Moon, J. (1991). The middle manager: Truly in the middle. In P. L Moore (Ed.), *Managing the political dimensions of student affairs* (New Directions for Student Services, No. 55, pp. 43–54). San Francisco, CA: Jossey-Bass.

Hemphill, B. O. (2012). Future leaders face shifting landscapes. *Leadership Exchange, 10*(1), 11–12.

Hernandez, C. L. (2010). *A case study exploring motivational determinants of mid-level student affairs administrators* (Unpublished doctoral dissertation). Texas A&M University, College Station, TX.

Hirt, J. (2006). *Where you work matters: Student affairs administration at different types of institutions.* Lanham, MD: University Press of America.

Hughes, C. (2004). Introduction to part 4. In K. Renn & C. Hughes (Eds.), *Roads taken: Women in student affairs at mid-career* (pp. 135–142). Sterling, VA: Stylus.

Johnsrud, L. K. (1996). *Maintaining morale: A guide to assessing the morale of midlevel administrators and faculty.* Washington, DC: College and University Personnel Association.

Johnsrud, L. K., Heck, R. H., & Rosser, V. J. (2000). Morale matters: Midlevel administrators and their intent to leave. *Journal of Higher Education, 71*(1), 34–59.

Komives, S. (1992). The middles: Observations on professional competence and autonomy. *NASPA Journal, 29*, 83–90.

Mills, D. B. (2000). The role of the middle manager. In M. Barr & M. Desler (Eds.), *The handbook of student affairs administration* (pp. 135–153). San Francisco, CA: Jossey-Bass.

Not alone: The first report of the White House Task Force to Protect Students from Sexual Assault. (2014). Retrieved from http://www.nsvrc.org/publications/reports/not-alone-first-report-white-house-task-force-protect-students-sexual-assault

Rosser, V. J. (2004). A national study on midlevel leaders in higher education: The unsung professionals in the academy. *Higher Education, 48*, 317–337.

Sagaria, M., & Johnsrud, L. K. (1988). Mobility within the student affairs profession: Career advancement through position change. *Journal of College Student Development, 29*(1), 30–40.

Scott, R. A. (1975). Middle management on campus: Training ground or wasteland. *Journal of the National Association of College Admissions Counselors, 20*(1), 38–40.

U.S. Department of Education. (2011, April 4). *Dear colleague letter: Sexual violence.* Retrieved from http://www2.ed.gov/about/offices/list/ocr/letters/colleague-201104.html

Violence Against Women Reauthorization Act of 2013, Title III, §304.

Young, R. B. (2001). Guiding values and philosophy. In S. Komives & D. Woodward (Eds.), *Student services: A handbook for the profession* (3rd ed., pp. 83–105). San Francisco, CA: Jossey-Bass.

Taking the Journey from AVP to VPSA

Levester Johnson and Joan L. Kindle

Some say that timing is everything. That might be true for many important decisions in life, including when to make the move to a chief student affairs position. Readiness for a position as vice president for student affairs (VPSA) involves serious introspection at both personal and professional levels.

To gain insight and advice, we interviewed six successful chief student affairs officers (CSAOs) about their professional journeys from associate/assistant vice president (AVP) to the top position. Collectively, the interviews uncovered that timing is part of the answer, but other factors are influential as well. The selected journeys represent a variety of personal backgrounds as well as institutional types and sizes; each one offers insight on such questions as: How do you know if or when it is time to consider a move to a VPSA position? What role does risk taking play in preparing for such a move? How do you weigh personal factors when faced with professional opportunity? What role do mentors play as you move from AVP to VPSA, and what assistance can they provide during and after the transition?

The journeys showcased in this chapter are part of complex, multifaceted, real-life stories. We focus on only a few golden nuggets from each story that might have particular relevance to those who are contemplating a professional transition to and through the AVP position in student affairs. The six CSAOs have agreed to use their real names and institutions in order to allow for follow-up questions from readers.

Each journey has examples of strategic thinking, risk taking, individual passions, effective mentoring, challenges, and difficult decisions. Each cautions that there are multiple pathways and no simple guide. The insight and relevance can be found by looking at the uniqueness of each journey.

- Frank Ross, vice president for student affairs at Northeastern Illinois University, knew what he wanted early in his career and smoothly navigated a strategic route to the AVP role and on to the VPSA position.
- Lori White, vice chancellor for students at Washington University in St. Louis, challenged traditional pathways to and through the AVP position.
- Les Cook, vice president for student affairs and advancement at Michigan Technological University, made a wrong move, but it strengthened his professional vision and guided him to a successful transition to the top.
- Anna Gonzalez, dean of students and chief student affairs officer at Lewis and Clark College, developed a strategic plan that aligned with her values, allowing her to market transferable skills into executive positions.

- Magdalena de la Teja, vice president for student development services at Tarrant County College–Northeast Campus, pursued a love of learning to complete a doctorate and law degree while she focused on service in the community college.
- Sarah Westfall, vice president for student development and dean of students at Kalamazoo College, followed her passion back to a small college environment where she began her own undergraduate experience.

I Always Knew

Some student affairs journeys are marked by a clear sense of direction, focus, and intentionality. This describes the path taken by Frank Ross III, whose executive roles at large public institutions led to his current position as VPSA at Northeastern Illinois University. With more than 20 years of experience, Frank has been meticulous and strategic in planning and seeking positions and leadership opportunities that have afforded him diverse experiences. Moving through academic affairs, enrollment management, adult education, and other areas outside the traditional student affairs portfolio, Frank knew the breadth of opportunities would assist him in securing a VPSA position.

Frank knew typical roles—fraternity and sorority advisor and associate director of campus and community life at large public universities—would serve as stepping stones to the VPSA role. In addition to completing some of the standard credentials leading to AVP and VPSA roles, such as a master's of education and student affairs and a doctorate, Frank also completed another master's degree in adult and community education. Obtaining this second master's degree while holding an assistantship as an academic adviser served as a pivotal moment in Frank's career journey.

The experience opened my eyes to what type of functional areas are possibilities for positively impacting student learning and engagement. It opened my eyes to student affairs functions housed within academic units (which was not as common back then) and the possibilities of true integration and collaboration between student affairs and academic affairs. The whole depth and breadth of higher education and the importance of the whole academy became more important and clearly defined.

After this "aha" moment Frank became more "bilingual." The experience provided him a whole new vocabulary and he began speaking the academic language, which he felt led to becoming a successful administrator. Frank also recognized his passion and the dedication he has for serving underrepresented populations within urban areas.

Frank fondly remembered taking on his first AVP role as assistant vice chancellor of student life at a large public institution located within a metropolitan area. Frank said that initial AVP roles were not as well-defined then as they are today, nor was there specific training and professional preparation for assuming the role. "In many ways, it was a mysterious and undefined role and not like other roles and positions, and clearly was never described in any graduate courses I took." Frank interviewed for this position as an internal applicant.

> It is challenging when you are going from a role as a peer to supervision of your peers as an internal candidate. You are instantly moving from operating at a micro level to that of a macro-level perspective, in a position overseeing multiple departments and with more responsibilities associated. The realization that this was truly a new and different experience came to me on day one during my first one-on-one meeting.

Frank freely acknowledges the important role mentors have played in his professional development, including those within academic affairs. One particular mentor was an academic dean of a college. Frank was holding a position that was funded jointly by academic affairs and student affairs. His mentor encouraged him to serve on academic committees; through that experience Frank realized, "At the end of the day, we serve the academic end of the institution, and understanding student learning outcomes has assisted in my development." Serving on an academic policies committee was the greatest learning experience in his career.

> When it came to creating policies for dropping students from courses or discontinuing financial aid, this was a wake-up call to the importance of certain fundamental work being done within universities that goes to the academic core of what we are about. Developing policies that affect the engagement and therefore retention of students was a significant aha moment.

Frank also credited both formal and informal mentors as critical in his professional and career development. While serving as an AVP, he sat at the table with administrators from a wide variety of areas throughout campus; he watched them make key institutional decisions and learned to emulate their strengths. He felt ready to make the move to CSAO when, while serving as AVP, he found himself constantly imagining how he would handle decisions if he were the VPSA. He finally reached a point where he was thinking and processing information "more like a person in a VPSA role than the AVP role I was holding."

In determining his move to a VPSA position, Frank stayed true to his values and passions. He has a commitment to access to education and social justice. Therefore, he intentionally and strategically placed himself into roles and institutional environments that serve underrepresented populations and urban metropolitan areas.

Frank is now in his second VPSA role. Whatever comes next, he keeps in mind an important question regardless of the role, "Are you still having fun?"

> If you are in an AVP role and it seems you have stopped having fun, ask yourself "Why is that?" It may be that you need to find something

to reignite your energy and that something may very well be taking that intentional step to the VPSA level.

Don't Box Me In

Several traditional paths lead to the senior position: the involved student leader mentored by the dean of students, or those who ascended through the ranks of a specific discipline—often the housing and residence life area. The journey of Lori White, vice chancellor for students at Washington University in St. Louis, is anything but traditional. Her path challenges preconceived notions regarding positions that limit career advancement and shows how roles that "box you in" can turn into an excellent foundation for the VPSA position.

From the start of her undergraduate experience, Lori was anything but the engaged coed who found her niche on campus thriving in student organizations, attending campus events, and immersing herself in campus traditions and activities. There was no student affairs practitioner noticing her talent and thus asking the stock question of student leaders: "Have you ever thought about going into student affairs?" Rather, Lori went to classes and focused on academics. Had it not been for her father serving as a faculty member at another institution and assisting her in landing her first post-college job on the campus where he worked, she would have never been introduced to the transformative power of student engagement and the student affairs professionals who often foster such environments.

The position her father helped secure was at the information booth within the student union on campus. By witnessing the daily comings and goings of students, faculty, staff, alumni, and campus visitors, she was introduced to student affairs professionals and able to witness their interactions and engagement with students. To her amazement, she discovered that "somehow students were getting connected through student affairs

Taking the Journey from AVP to VPSA 181

professionals"—something she had not experienced or realized she was missing. It was through this first campus job that she became connected with some of those professionals and developed a greater understanding of the transformative power of student engagement and administrative work within higher education.

Even with this knowledge and increased understanding of the profession, Lori did not follow the traditional route and seek out a master's program in higher education administration. No, not Lori: Don't box her in! After graduating with her bachelor's in psychology and English and with the knowledge gained from working in the campus information booth, she forged right into a professional position as a counselor and program assistant within a student affairs division at a large public university. This experience provided her a bird's-eye view of student affairs. During her 10-year tenure at this institution, she saw herself as a "student affairs professional who happened to work in different student affairs offices, and therefore a generalist." Moving from counselor and program assistant, to director of cross-cultural programs, to complex coordinator within university housing, and then back to director of cross-cultural programs offered Lori valuable and varied experiences, stretching her knowledge and skill boundaries while she worked at the same institution.

With a desire to advance her career opportunities while embracing the philosophy of "go out and get the most powerful credential you can," Lori sought additional knowledge within higher education administration. Lori set off to complete her doctorate in higher education administration and policy analysis at a large, prestigious, tier-one research institution. She skipped right past the master's degree. Don't box her in!

Lori's first job after completing graduate school was at a midsize private institution as the director of student programs. This position lasted only a year, because she was quickly recruited back to the university where she received her doctorate, this time within the academic area by serving as assistant and then associate vice provost for undergraduate education and director of undergraduate advising. For 6 years, she focused on undergraduate advising, curriculum development, general education requirements, faculty priorities, and the potential for academic and student affairs collaboration. She then realized that she had advanced as far as she could on the academic side. Ascending to the role of provost was less likely without a solid research and teaching background as a tenured faculty member at this institution, and she knew she would need to transition back to student affairs.

This decision led to her first AVP role at another large state institution as the associate vice president for student affairs and dean of students. The move also expanded her experience, because she went from a well-endowed institution plentiful in resources to "an environment facing the challenges of finding resources." While managing multiple areas, she began to realize that

> people were mentoring me. I guess I would call them "earth angels in my life" before I even knew they were mentoring me! They really uncovered my strength in creating relationships and helped me network with people. I would not be where I am today without mentors.

By leveraging her networking skills, she found other seasoned practitioners mentoring her and opening doors for her, even if for the benefit of their own institution and operations. It was just 2 years before a bartering war began between the VPSA for her current institution and a VPSA mentor from another institution within the same state. Ultimately, she took that next step in professional development and left for the new role at the second institution, which was a large private institution. This position was her second role as an AVP for student affairs.

Lori loved her job. The position once again provided the opportunity to supervise a number of different areas and even a few outside normal student affairs portfolios, such as campus recreation as well as a stint as the interim director of the Black alumni association. She also had the chance to learn about leadership from a strategic perspective. Lori considered herself the epitome of what an AVP should be.

> Your job is to please the VPSA. You have less independence. You are the representative of the VPSA and thus to a certain extent, think like your VPSA. The most difficult thing I had to do in this role was place my ego aside. I knew I needed to do whatever was needed to support the VPSA.

In time she became very content in this role and was extremely good at it. The next challenge came when Lori's mentors told her she needed to be a VPSA, but Lori couldn't see it. She could not envision herself taking that next step into the VPSA role. Luckily for Lori, one of her mentors challenged her on such a linear perspective of looking forward by saying, "Lori, it's a good thing you are this way, always looking forward, but be careful: There may be opportunities off to the side that you may never see." This was Lori's "aha" moment, and, because she was in a relationship with someone on the opposite coast, she took the advice, expanded her scope of opportunities, and made that move to the VPSA level.

> Sometimes mentors will tell you it's time to take the step up and are invested in helping you get there. When you do outstanding work where you are, people will reward you for your good work. It's all right to be mindful of "shining" for the great work that you do, but you also need to be intentional with your supervisors and mentors about identifying experiences that will assist you in reaching that next level.

Having made the decision to pursue a VPSA position, Lori sought out institutions where she could "safely test the waters" by focusing on the types of universities where she had been highly successful. "Over time, hopefully, we all figure out what institution type has worked best for us." Pursuing the VPSA role at Southern Methodist University (SMU) was of interest to Lori for her first VPSA position because the environment was similar to universities where she had previously worked and its medium size would afford the opportunities to continue having significant student contact. "Knowing myself and what motivates me, I thought SMU offered the best fit for me for my first VPSA position."

In offering advice for AVPs who are considering making the move to the VPSA level, Lori suggests not being afraid to take that leap when you are ready.

> Find a place where you can safely test the water, but also don't be afraid to go for the next, or "stretch," position. Even if you don't get it, it might serve you well for the position you ultimately interview for and achieve.

She also cautions that you should not get caught up in the idea that only certain tracks or positions lead to the VPSA role. Her career track challenges the notion that it is difficult to move to the VPSA ranks from a background in diversity programs. Although she was conscious of the amount of time she spent as director of multicultural affairs, Lori cited the experience as the most significant in preparing her for the VPSA role.

All the skills I use every day came from my experience as a director of multicultural affairs: how to be an advocate for students within a university administrative role, how to manage conflict, how to build bridges that go both ways, and how to manage and provide services with minimum fiscal resources.

Lori's path to the VPSA role can be summed up as "the road least traveled" and serves as an inspirational testimony for an AVP prepared to challenge conventional thinking or career paths and who refuse to be "boxed in." In 2015, Lori accepted her second CSAO role as the vice chancellor for students at Washington University in St. Louis.

Taking the Journey from AVP to VPSA 185

I Took a Wrong Turn

Strategic planning provides a guide for making decisions along your professional journey. However, when the unexpected happens, you can find yourself in the wrong place. Les Cook is the vice president for student affairs and advancement and adjunct professor of education at Michigan Technological University. He has held the VPSA role since 2004. From the outside, his professional journey seems like a direct trajectory, from orientation roles as an undergraduate, to assistant director of admissions, to director of orientation and leadership, to AVP for student life, and on to the VPSA. A closer look reveals a professional journey that teaches the importance of taking a risk to leave a position when professional fit is missing and having the tenacity to keep moving forward without job security. Les described his journey to the AVP role as "taking the wrong turn and trying to find a new route back to the highway."

Before pursuing the AVP role, Les finished his doctorate and worked for 6 years at a large public research university in Utah at the director level in orientation and leadership. He had 15 years of post-master's-degree experience. His professional positions in Utah progressed in title and breadth of responsibilities. From the beginning of his career, Les complemented his professional experiences with active participation in NASPA and other organizations. He held roles as conference chair, regional board member, and network chair prior to applying for AVP positions. Through NASPA affiliations and his work at the university, Les had developed a network of mentors whom he used in developing a strong professional reputation in the field. Things looked promising, and the path to a VPSA position was mapping out nicely. Les was encouraged by others and felt confident that he was ready for an AVP role.

An advertisement for an AVP position in a different state caught his eye. He connected with mentors and those he knew who had previously worked at the institution. The feedback was all positive. Les' experiences aligned with the responsibilities of the new role, and he felt an AVP position at this institution would be a good fit for him. Shortly after his application, he interviewed and was offered the job. He discussed the offer with his family. They agreed to make the move; his wife closed her business, they put their home on the market, and the children settled into new schools. With positive anticipation, Les began his first job as an AVP. Within a few months on the new job, Les knew he had to leave.

What happened? Les discovered that what seemed like a perfect fit from the outside was not enough to be successful. Relevant professional experiences that aligned with the job responsibilities helped prepare him to transition to the new duties, but that was not enough. He had researched the move from public to private higher education and received plenty of feedback from mentors and colleagues about the institution's cultural fit, but that was not enough. Les inherited a team open to working together on strategic planning and setting new directions—encouraging, but not enough. The professional fit between him and the VPSA was stalling progress. Clear expectations, partnering to set goals and targets, and work-style preferences were either missing or not aligning. The connection between the VPSA and the AVP is critical to success. It is not about being right or wrong; it is about connecting as a team, and complementary styles are important. In retrospect, Les believes that he did not know enough about his VPSA's working style, and the VPSA did not know enough about his style before he made the decision.

With an organizational structure that had only one AVP position, Les felt disconnected and frustrated without a strong, comfortable working relationship. Efforts to better align expectations and styles did not improve matters. He knew that he needed to leave, but timing was paramount. He had fewer than 4 months on the job. Adding to the mix, Les was dealing with personal factors: He had just uprooted his family, had sold his home in Utah, was in the process of building a new home, and his wife had left her family business behind. It was taking a psychological and physical toll. "It was one of those things where every night you wake up and your heart is racing and you cannot sleep, and you begin to think, what have I done?"

Serving as chair of the NASPA Region IV-East Conference that year, Les used the opportunity to once again seek the advice of his mentors, some of whom had encouraged him to apply for the AVP position. They advised him to negotiate a settlement and leave the position. They also encouraged him to rely on the depth of his previous experiences that gave him professional credibility. He discovered that finding yourself at a professional dead-end is not uncommon. Through the experience, he learned that dwelling on the negative outcome was not getting him anywhere. He needed to focus on moving forward—finding his way back on the highway. Les negotiated an amicable release and settlement. He realized that leaving was in the best interest of both parties. Les was now without a job and in need of a plan.

Figuring out a new direction is not an easy task. Even with support in his personal life and mentors who offered him opportunities to do consulting work, Les faced serious questions about himself and his future. "My self-worth took a tumble. I uprooted my family, did not have a house, and neither of us had jobs. Did I just throw everything away?" He did some deep soul searching and questioned his career direction. "What should I do with my life? Am I in the right field? Is higher education the answer?" He moved through the difficult evaluative and reflective aftermath of the experience with the help of family, colleagues, and mentors. He came to the realization that his professional journey was not a mistake, even with this wrong turn. A mistake does not define the professional; how you learn from mistakes is the defining element. Les knew he had to come to terms with his bruised ego and move through it. Reflecting back, Les said that belief in yourself is critical when dealing with the difficulties in the journey. To prove the point and with a bit of irony, Les received NASPA's regional and national Mid-Level Professional Award that year, even though he did not actually have a job at the time.

Battling the fear of the unknown is a constant when you face important decisions. Les said that "the best advice is to not be risk adverse." When confronted with a work environment that is not the right fit, take on the challenge and do not be stopped by fear. "Enjoy the adventure," he advises. Be cautious but do not be stymied by the unknown, because the adventure brings unexpected opportunities to life. For Les, the experience helped his family grow stronger and be more appreciative of time together. They created some rich, life-long memories that they would have missed if he hadn't taken that wrong turn. Les also used the time to be more reflective about his options and researching for the next job.

In the job hunt process, Les was advised to be honest and forthright about his "wrong turn." The AVP position was listed on his résumé. He indicated that he had resigned due to a lack of professional fit. Les focused on hidden opportunities in what may have seemed like a poor career move. He put what he learned from the experience into the fuller context of his 15-year career and began looking for AVP, dean of students, and larger director roles. He wanted to move forward and build on his director-level experiences in orientation and leadership. Les also noted that he realized he had an advantage in having had a joint reporting relationship to an academic AVP and a student affairs AVP when he was the director of orientation and leadership development. Additionally, he had adjunct teaching experience. Having experience with academic affairs was a unique factor that helped him in the next job hunt. According to Les, those who are moving to and through AVP roles should look for ways to gain experience across academic and student affairs lines.

Les referred to NASPA as his "personal job search firm." When he searched for his next job, he called on his professional colleagues to help identify and research potential positions. Les had invested in his professional membership in NASPA over the years, and the return proved invaluable. He advises AVPs to get involved in a professional association of their choice in order to create a network of valuable colleagues for support.

Les approached the next set of interviews with a sharper focus on listening. Adhering to the adage "look before you leap," he stressed the need to take hard, honest looks before making decisions. The interview process is filled with the anticipation and excitement, and these emotions can overshadow the facts. Do not be swayed by what you want to hear. "Listen with excitement but also with an earnest ear for the real messages being given." He spent more time asking questions and getting to know the people he met. Les also continued to use his mentors and colleagues who currently or previously worked at the institutions where he interviewed. This time, he asked more questions about the working style and institutional culture than he did previously.

Receiving three offers, Les involved his family to be certain that the next location was the right fit for everyone. In the end, Les accepted an offer at Michigan Technological University as the vice provost for student affairs and dean of students and adjunct associate professor of education. In this position he reported to the provost and senior vice president for academic and student affairs. He sensed the right fit when he began his new position. Michigan Tech was seeking to revitalize student affairs and Les was looking for a place where he could focus on strategic planning and implement new approaches and ideas. Les recalled that "the provost gave me the space I needed to grow, but also the encouragement I needed to be successful."

After the wrong turn, Les found his way back and moved his career forward. Even with forward motion, unexpected things happen. Within a year of accepting the vice provost position at Michigan Tech, the president moved on; an academic dean was made the president and reorganization ensued. Les moved to the direct reporting line to the president and became the VPSA within 9 months.

Twelve years later, Les still adheres to the lessons he learned when he veered off track. He says that it is critical to believe in yourself even when the professional journey is not smooth. Les encourages new AVPs to keep sight of what they love to do. "If the situation is not going well and there is no opportunity to correct it, face it and move through it with professionalism." Opportunities to learn and grow as a professional can come from situations that seem far from ideal. His best advice is to not be risk adverse. Go for it. Avoid the "should haves" by embracing the opportunities. "You have to be willing to risk and enjoy the ride—even the twists and turns."

I Stayed True to Myself

Personal experiences often shape the direction of a professional journey. Anna Gonzalez, dean of students and VPSA at Lewis and Clark College, developed a strategic professional plan that aligned with her core values and passions. Anna assumed the VPSA position at Lewis and Clark in 2012. She moved into the chief officer role at a small private college in Oregon after holding the AVP role at a large public research university in Illinois for 4 years. With 20 years of experience in higher education, she has intentionally sought out professional opportunities that have allowed her to pursue her specialization in diversity education and switch between large and small institutions while still progressing into executive-level positions. Her journey as a woman of color, an immigrant, a first-generation college graduate, and a highly respected leader in higher education is marked with lessons about following passions, listening to mentors, being strategic, learning to say no, and finding her unique balance in life.

Be strategic and make an intentional plan for the future. Anna cautions to never stay in a job when it gets too easy or when decisions become instinctive rather than fresh. These lessons were learned while spending 15 years at a large public research university in California. She started as program coordinator for a multicultural center and progressed to the associate dean of students managing centers and services for various student populations. It was her passion and life's work. Although she loved the job and the institution, Anna thought she was getting too comfortable and feared she may one day utter, "That's not the way we do things here." Her institution offered no open options for promotion; it was time to leave. Anna's advice is to not get too comfortable; take the risk to seek new opportunities. In retrospect, she thinks she may have stayed too long, but she learned the value of having a personal strategic plan. "As things unfold, deviations from the plan may occur"—but being intentional about decisions kept her eye on the future.

Anna made a big move in leaving her California roots for an AVP role in the Midwest. She built on her passion for and expertise in cross-cultural programming as she moved into the associate vice chancellor role at a large public research university in Illinois. She focused on policy development that supports diversity and those practices that address the needs of diverse student populations. The AVP role reinvigorated Anna, and she was able to continue her specialist focus as well as move to a policy-level position. She advises those in specialist career paths: Be sure to gain other experiences that afford an understanding of institutionwide operations and issues by participating in institutionwide committee service and getting involved with issues that impact higher education on the professional-association level. She stated that combining the expertise of the specialist with institutionwide perspectives enhances the transition to executive-level positions.

While in the AVP role, Anna was completing her dissertation. Her one regret is that she did not take enough time to enjoy the writing process. Her new AVP role involved policy research and reform. The combination of this role with her dissertation work made it difficult to appreciate the process. She advises others to take the time to enjoy the doctoral process before getting consumed in a new position.

Strong mentors are credited for stepping in and challenging Anna to stretch her vision of the future. They encouraged her to pursue a doctoral degree and to seek an AVP role. Anna continues to reach out to others for advice and she listens. "I have been lucky to get connected with so many mentors in my life." Anna encourages others to follow through when experienced professionals extend business cards or offer to assist in some way. Anna makes a point of contacting these people in her life and maintaining the connection. When she reads an interesting book in her graduate classes, she contacts the author to get more information and to make a connection. Through her affiliations with NASPA, she has developed a network of mentors who are VPSAs and leaders in the profession. These contacts helped as she sought the AVP role and her subsequent move to the VPSA spot. Through these connections, she was recommended for leadership roles in NASPA where she has directed several institutes and chaired conferences and program boards. Anna encourages others to intentionally seek out people who can mentor and assist throughout the career lifetime.

As noted, Anna believes in developing strategic plans when it comes to your career. A big part of the strategy is staying true to yourself and your core beliefs. Being the first in her family to be educated in the United States, Anna credits them for encouraging and supporting her education. Her personal experience with strong family involvement helped her understand the hardship that first-generation families experience when children leave home to attend college. Her family also supported Anna in attending private schools that stressed the value of service. "Men and women for others" is the Jesuit value she embraced. Servant leadership is part of who she is and the value that directs her work. Her experience as an immigrant from the Philippines influences her ability to understand students in transition and is core to her mission to improve the student experience. Anna advises to be introspective and clear about the values that drive you forward. A career path that aligns with your core values is essential in being able to handle the challenges that arise along the way.

Anna recognized that her policy work in a large state university system positively addressed student issues. However, she missed being a part of individual student experiences that were at the core of her values. Anna knew that mission-driven institutions and smaller college environments could afford her deeper connections and a greater impact on students. "I missed seeing my impact directly with students—not only from 50,000 feet above." She developed her next strategic move in accordance with these values. Anna had to be prepared to address why a switch from a large public university to a small private institution was the right move. "I came from a small university and wanted go back to where I was first inspired as an undergraduate to go into student affairs. I told my dean of students, 'I want to have your job someday.'" She advises others considering a switch to a different institutional type to be clear about where they thrive best. Limit choices to those types of institutions and positions that best match your self-identity. She cautions against applying for jobs with desirable titles but poor institutional fit. Anna believes that candidates must be able to articulate where and why they would be successful in a specific institutional environment, particularly when moving to the top position. The alignment between her values and the mission of the institution was a top priority in considering the VPSA position at Lewis and Clark College. Introspection into her values and experiences allowed her to demonstrate that this move was not only strategic but personally aligned.

Anna also offered advice about seeking a doctorate. She believes that this degree has given her entrance into the faculty ranks and helped her in building partnerships with faculty colleagues. At Lewis and Clark, she helped develop the master's program in student affairs and she holds rank as assistant professor. Because she has experience within as well as outside the classroom, she has been able to participate more fully in the academy as a VPSA.

Finding balance between work and personal life is also essential. Anna and her husband are dual-career educators, administrators and tenured faculty members. Both are committed to their careers and have found a balance point that works. Capitalizing on the flexibility of faculty class schedules and carving out long stretches of time during vacations, breaks, holidays, and sabbaticals, the couple has been able to create a balance that fits. Once again, Anna's advice is that one size does not fit all. In trying to find the balance in life, you need to respect personal values, know where compromise is possible, and align decisions to match.

When asked what her best advice is for those moving to and through the AVP role, Anna's response was direct: Learn how and when to say no. "Make when you say yes matter by giving meaningful no's." As a new AVP or VPSA, the desire to help and to be liked can cloud good decision making. Making exceptions and stepping over rules set precedence and ultimately are not sustainable. In her AVP role, Anna learned this lesson the hard way. Some people expected Anna to bend the rules just because she could identify with them or understand their situations. These leadership roles are not popularity contests; they require the ability to make hard decisions. Everyone cannot get everything. Consistency, clear rationales, and a focus on the big picture are key to effectively saying yes or no.

As you move to and through the AVP role, listening is key. Anna believes in listening to yourself and to those true mentors who can say what you need to hear. Develop a career strategy that embraces your true self and targets positions that can empower you through an alignment with your core values.

I Was Called

With a life-long passion to increase access to high-quality education for the underrepresented and economically disadvantaged, Magdalena (Maggie) H. de la Teja set her sights on preparing for a career in community college leadership. Maggie is the vice president for student development services at Tarrant County College–Northeast Campus in Fort Worth, Texas. As a first-generation Latina college graduate, Maggie knew firsthand the community college environment serves as the on-ramp to postsecondary education. Maggie went on to complete a succession of degrees, including a bachelor's, master's, doctorate, and law degree from a large research university in Texas. Her interest in student affairs began as an active student leader and was nurtured by the university president and other professionals who spotted her passion for increasing access for underrepresented populations. When she decided to pursue her doctorate, she selected the community college leadership focus. Maggie began her journey from a student development specialist to an administrative intern for the president and then to the AVP role at her alma mater.

Maggie knew that she wanted to work to improve student access, but she did not start out with a goal to be a VPSA in the community college. "I let my passions lead me." Her involvement in student activities and leadership opportunities made her aware of the important connection between student engagement and success. Her own involvement began to shape the direction of her career. Without knowing her ultimate goal, Maggie set out to gain the educational preparation that could serve her well into the future, wherever that might lead. She was committed to a challenging educational path and achieved four degrees in 13 years. Maggie developed strong working relationships with those in student affairs while she was an undergraduate student leader and an employee right before entering her doctoral program. Her passion for working with underrepresented populations became widely known. In turn, the professionals at the university noticed Maggie's potential and helped launch her career. "It was an opportune time that I didn't expect."

After completing her master's degree in communications, she was hired as a student development specialist at the same university. Maggie encourages others to be introspective and follow their own passions. Her experiences as an undergraduate leader, her work at the university union, and her passion for working with underrepresented student populations directed her path into higher education leadership. She decided to pursue her doctorate while working in student development. Her mentors encouraged her to pursue university-level administration, but Maggie specifically selected the community college leadership track. She had worked only at the university level, but she decided that someday she would like to be at a community college working to open educational doors for other underrepresented and economically disadvantaged students. With an eye on the future, Maggie started to gain educational and work experiences that would best prepare her. She encourages others to "make decisions that fit into your own value system and what kind of life you want." As she finished her doctorate, she continued to focus on gaining valuable experiences that would benefit her long-term career in higher education. The university president was interested in having Maggie help expand underrepresented student access and asked her to work as a presidential intern, which led to her entry into the AVP role at the university.

As she entered the AVP role, Maggie was encouraged by her mentors to pursue her interest in law. When asked about her decision to pursue a law degree after her doctorate, she indicated that it was all about following her interests. She enjoyed a previous law course and knew that she wanted to pursue a law degree at some future point. Her alma mater again helped make the timing right, and she entered law school. "I was strategically trying to prepare myself for the future. I thought I would be more marketable with a doctorate and law degree. The law is important to our work in student affairs in a lot of different ways." Although she does not recommend it, Maggie went to law school while being a full-time AVP; she completed her degree in 3 years.

Maggie was able to satisfy her thirst for education and launch her student affairs career at the same institution of higher education. Staying at the same institution allowed her to focus on her education while gaining experience. Within 13 years, Maggie not only completed four degrees but also held progressively more responsible professional positions that included 5 years as the AVP. After completing her law degree, Maggie thought it would be helpful to her future to obtain practical experience as an attorney. She left university life and worked for 3 years with the Texas Legislative Council gaining experience in researching and writing proposed legislation concerning higher education. However, she did not lose focus on her ultimate goal of moving to the community college setting. Within 3 years, she accepted a director position that was upgraded to the campus dean of student services in a large community college district in the Southwest. With a doctorate in community college leadership and a law degree, combined with her 5 years as an AVP, Maggie's transition to the VPSA position was smooth.

Professional journeys typically include tough choices and risks. Maggie recognizes that it is hard to step out of your comfort zone and jump into something unknown or less secure. She encourages others to surround themselves with colleagues and family who support them. Based on her own experiences, Maggie encourages others to reach out and find ways to partner on ideas, presentations, and publications at every stage. Maggie joined NASPA when very few community college professionals were members. She became active in establishing community college representation on the board and bringing community college issues to the forefront. Maggie helped pave the way for other community college professionals. In return, Maggie found a professional home and colleagues with whom she can share ideas, collaborate on projects, and commiserate.

Maggie also faced a tough decision when a VPSA role opened in the Tarrant County College District in the Fort Worth area. Taking this VPSA position meant moving away from her family in Austin. The decision was eased by the support of her husband and adult children. She and her family have found a way to make this work successfully. She cautions that making the right decision requires personal introspection and an understanding of how your circumstances change throughout a lifetime.

Maggie's educational journey led her back to the community college setting where she has been a VPSA for 26 years as a dean and vice president. Maggie believes in paying it forward. She believes her life-changing experiences as a student—engaged in activities and supported by strong mentors—opened the world of educational opportunities for her. She credits her successful career path to her own excitement for learning and her passion for helping other students. Becoming a leader in community colleges was a way for her to cultivate that thirst for knowledge in others and to open doors of opportunity for many.

I Returned to the Water

After an adult female sea turtle leaves the water to nest her eggs, she returns to the water. She leaves her nest and soon-to-be baby turtles, or hatchlings, to follow suit and come to the water as well. This full cycle, or returning to your roots, is the career path of Sarah Westfall in landing her first VPSA position at a small institution as vice president for student development and dean of students at Kalamazoo College. Her affinity and love for the small college environment began during her undergraduate days at a small private Midwestern liberal arts university with 2,000 students. You can hear the excitement in her voice recounting the engaging undergraduate experience she had serving as a resident assistant and other leadership roles. Here she saw that student affairs practitioners had the opportunity for significant engagement and daily contact with students while they also addressed strategic initiatives for their institution.

Sarah felt particularly fortunate that many student affairs professionals at the institution took her under their wings by serving as mentors and providing numerous opportunities to interact with faculty and other administrators through institutional committees. She began thinking about graduate school during her sophomore year. The dean of students, who was not only an influential higher education practitioner for their campus but a pioneer within the student affairs profession as a whole, became her mentor and paved the way for numerous young professionals along the way. The commitment to pursuing the profession did not occur until her junior year. "I can remember clearly the day, walking into my residence hall where I served as an RA [resident advisor], when I got a strange sense, an epiphany, that working within the university environment and serving students was my calling."

After graduation, Sarah pursued a master's in a college student personnel program at a large public university in the Midwest. Upon receipt of her degree, she took her first professional position by returning to a small private Midwestern college as assistant dean of students for several years. This college proved to be a challenging environment, because students and parents were significantly engaged and involved with the educational experience, which Sarah described as having some "real intensity." Sarah valued the experience and felt she learned a great deal, coming away "better prepared for working with parents."

Sarah always knew that she wanted to be a dean of students. She had seen an extraordinary dean of students in action during her undergraduate days. She had also heard from her mentors that earning her doctorate would be important in paving this way. A doctorate would provide credibility among the faculty and academic colleagues in serving "like a union card," according to Sarah. She felt it would provide even more value within the small school environment. Sarah said that "the earlier the degree can be acquired, the better; also, the less complicated your life, the better." Taking her own advice and that of her mentors, she entered the doctoral program in higher education at Indiana University.

After completing her doctorate, Sarah sought a new challenge and took on a position at a branch campus of a large technical community college located within a metropolitan area. This environment was a professional stretch, beyond the traditional residential college students. Sarah's new role as coordinator of admission and financial aid gave her significant experience working with first-generation and nontraditional students. "I learned so much about these populations, and the experience expanded my knowledge of student services and breadth of the students we serve." This community college experience and the subsequent role as director of freshmen interest groups at a large public institution reconfirmed her affinity for the small collegiate environment and a feeling that her skills and strengths would be maximized and better used within these campus environments. Sarah has no regrets from taking on these roles: "I feel like it worked for me. I knew there was no magical path leading to the VPSA role, so I would not have done things differently if I had the chance to do it all again."

In her first return to the water—the small school environment—Sarah secured a position as associate dean of students at a small private liberal arts institution of just more than 2,000 students. This role led to her internal promotion to her first AVP role as dean of students within this same institution. While serving as the number two, she took on "the hard stuff," dealing with student deaths and developing new services and programs for international students. Sarah was always ready to take on what the institution needed and wasn't afraid of experiences and opportunities to develop new skills. She firmly believes that "if you are committed and honest, good things will come your way and unexpected opportunities occur. When these opportunities come your way, you should take them."

Having served at this institution for a total of 6 years, Sarah decided it was time to make that transition to a VPSA role.

> The last few years I had given what I could give to that role and in return I had received a lot from it, but I began feeling restless. I felt fortunate working at this institution, but could not see what was next for me there. Basically, I felt I had mastered the dean's role.

Sarah's affiliation with a national professional association played an important role in pursuing a VPSA position. Sarah consulted with her friends and colleagues who were also committed to serving small colleges and universities. Some of these colleagues served as mentors, providing the challenge and support needed for professional development along the way. Sarah referred to her mentors as:

> "I think you should try this" type of mentors—people who took notice of my capacity and were generous with their time with me. Nothing prepared me better than these caring mentors who constantly put things in front of me, sort of sticking the right ottoman in front of me so I would encounter the things that I would not have encountered otherwise. They tended to my needs based on my aspirational goals.

Sarah completed an assessment of her own skills and background, including competencies in which she considered herself more secure and others in which she felt less secure. Sarah then went through a process of reviewing VPSA position descriptions, "trying on" positions by comparing herself with the requisite competencies and skills. When Sarah considered VPSA roles within small colleges and universities, she realized that position titles often take on greater meaning than in larger universities. "The portfolio and reporting line is even more important at small colleges. It was very important for me to find positions that reported to the president."

Probably the most critical consideration centered on the fact that Sarah is openly lesbian. High on her list of "musts" for campus environments was being valued within the community and that all aspects of her were validated.

> At first, early on in my professional track, I was most concerned with questions like "Where was I going to be safe? Where can I work in a secure way?" Later on in my career, it became more important to pursue places where the values of the workplace support me. A domestic-partner policy at larger institutions may have been better, but I have been able to be selective because of my values and priorities and been able to find those small schools that were able to provide the needed support and value.

Sarah said that one of the magical things about higher education is the variety of institutions. "I encourage colleagues to have hope and not stereotype small colleges, that there is variety and opportunity there and to seek a match with those types of institutions as well." Therefore, if you've ever experienced the intimacy and engagement offered by small campuses across the country or have been introduced to them through a colleague, mentor, or network, Sarah and her other small institution practitioners invite you to imagine yourself as the small turtle and return to the water!

Conclusion

Clearly, the journey toward a VPSA role is not one dimensional but a multifaceted experience involving complex career and personal decisions along the way. The six journeys showcased in this chapter not only offer nuggets that are particular to each practitioner but also point to themes that connect the experiences. While navigating the journey to the VPSA role, consider the following:

Take risks or a leap of faith. Most paths described in this chapter included a time when someone faced a significantly tough decision. You may encounter experiences in which you realize you have taken on a position that is the wrong fit, or you find yourself at an institution that does not match your desired passion for working with a particular population of students. Don't be afraid to embrace the experience for what it can offer you at the time and make the tough decision to move toward the next great opportunity.

Acquire cross-functional experiences. Achieving an understanding of, and experiences across, the functional areas of higher education is critical on the path to the VPSA role. Effectiveness as an executive is dependent on having a global perspective. In reaching the AVP role, you have probably broadened your portfolio and scope of responsibility along the way, but now challenge yourself to take on experiences within functional areas that may not be typical of student affairs. Serve on institutional committees that stretch your knowledge base, seek additional degrees that match a particular competency, or work on projects that embrace your passion for supporting student life and student learning.

Get experience in academic affairs. Clear and commanding knowledge of the workings of the institution and higher education is critical for taking on the VPSA role. Teaching and learning are the primary function, and thus experience and knowledge of the functions within this area are fundamental in an executive role as part of a team leading an institution. Stretch yourself: Serve on academic committees, take positions with direct lines of report or collaboration with academic affairs, or seek out mentors within academic affairs. You advance your chances of securing a VPSA role if you are "bilingual," able to speak the language of your academic colleagues.

Declare your preference. When you are weighing career experiences, your strengths within competencies, and simply your happiest positions in the past, it is perfectly acceptable to declare a particular institution type, student population, urban or rural environment, or other criteria as your professional niche. Doing so better assures a match between you and the institution.

Connect with mentors. Both formal and informal mentors can serve you in significant ways. They might challenge you to stretch your vision by placing the right "ottoman" in front of you to consider opportunities you otherwise would have passed on or by providing sound advice when you've made a wrong turn or choice. Make sure to have these "earth angels" by your side or a quick call away to guide you toward the VPSA position.

Align a career plan with core values. Understanding your core values and the passions that drive you forward are critical to making career decisions that fit. Don't be shortsighted or swayed by important-sounding titles. Focusing on institutional fit by investigating culture, work styles, missions, and other environmental factors prior to making a decision helps avoid a wrong turn. It also helps in developing a strategic plan that propels you to the VPSA role while staying aligned with personal values.

Create supportive networks. As you determine your passions and declare your preferences, look for professional associations or groups and the networks within them to further create a supportive circle of friends and colleagues. They can open doors to future VPSA roles that match your passion and preferences while providing knowledge on best practices within your shared area of interest.

Pursue credentials. All six VPSAs experienced pivotal points where a decision was made to pursue a doctorate or other credentials to bolster their candidacy for securing a VPSA position. Each pursued the most powerful credential possible both to gain expertise and knowledge of the profession and also to serve as that "union card" for academic colleagues. Other credentials, such as law degrees, MBAs, and certificate programs (e.g., Harvard's Management Development Program) can confer additional clout. Simply put, if you are intent on pursuing the VPSA position, credentials beyond a master's degree are highly recommended, and the doctorate is practically a must.

The journeys of these six VPSAs support the notion that timing is everything and confirm that no two journeys are the same. If you are an AVP considering the move to the VPSA role, consider these experiences as you develop a career strategy of your very own. So, what are you waiting for? Take the risk, make the leap, and join us in embracing one of the most rewarding roles within higher education as a VPSA.

Appendix A

AVP Checklist for Success

The first year in the AVP role is a critical time to learn your divisional and campus culture, build trust with your supervisor and staff, and make progress on your goals. Keep this checklist in a visible place on your desk as you move through the first few phases of your onboarding process.

30 Days (Or More) Before the Start Date:

- Schedule a phone call with your supervisor to get a brief overview of current issues within the division and to better understand the campus climate you will be entering.
- Reach out to each direct report to start building lines of communication.
- Read the divisional and university end-of-year reports to understand operational achievements and priorities.
- Review the university's strategic plan to identify overarching priorities and locate your division and departments in the plan.
- Request the general budget for the division and your specific area to familiarize yourself with the fiscal landscape of your portfolio.
- Request that your email and university access to files be granted prior to your start date so you can hit the ground running.
- Review the organizational chart for the division and consider how the organizational logic affects the student as well as the professional experience.

First 30 Days:

- Meet with your supervisor to review the short- and long-term priorities that define your role and to learn about the current hot-button issues.
- Find out your supervisor's expectations from you regarding communication (verbal, written, email, meetings, etc.).
- Meet with your direct reports individually. Review their résumés and most recent performance appraisals.
- Bring all direct reports together to discuss general supervisory expectations and the vision for moving forward together.
- Meet with key stakeholders inside and outside the division to understand the campus stories that shape the institutional culture.
- Meet with your administrative staff member (if applicable) to discuss expectations for managing your calendar and how this person can support you in this role.

Between 30 and 90 Days:

- Conduct a thorough review of each unit that reports to you to understand the mission, goals, and budgetary realities.
- Meet with your chief financial officer to better understand how money is raised and dispersed throughout the institution.
- Make a short list of strategic initiatives that you will work on in your first year.
- Develop a 1-year professional development plan based on the unique challenges and opportunities of your portfolio and campus climate.
- Develop a network of other student affairs AVPs, regionally and nationally, whom you can contact for advice and to share resources.

Appendix B

AVP Self-Assessment

The AVP role is fundamentally different and carries with it specific skills and competencies necessary for success. This self-assessment tool, based on the AVP competencies, is intended to help you identify your level of mastery within each area. Using the rating scale, answer each question based on your current level of skill or comfort. Being honest with your assessments will help you identify a baseline for your skills and abilities.

0 = No experience	1 = Disagree	2 = Agree	3 = Strongly agree	n/a = Not applicable to current position

Politics: Establishing important relationships and navigating the political arena of the institution and community.

1.	I can identify key stakeholders for my areas of responsibility.		0 1 2 3 n/a
2.	I am knowledgeable about the formal power structures at my institution.		0 1 2 3 n/a
3.	I have strong relationships with key leaders, both positional and influential.		0 1 2 3 n/a
4.	I directly involve stakeholders on critical initiatives for the division.		0 1 2 3 n/a
5.	I know who the informal leaders and influencers are on campus.		0 1 2 3 n/a
6.	I interact regularly with community leaders.		0 1 2 3 n/a
7.	I collaborate regularly with community members on issues important to the city, town, or community.		0 1 2 3 n/a

Position Skills: Developing the basic competencies to perform the AVP role.

8.	I know the skills critical to effective performance as an AVP.		0 1 2 3 n/a
9.	I can effectively teach these skills to others and do so via training and presentations.		0 1 2 3 n/a

10.	I am comfortable performing the duties of the VPSA in his or her absence.	0 1 2 3 n/a
11.	I have attended training sessions or institutes to better understand the AVP role.	0 1 2 3 n/a

Human Resources: Understanding team dynamics, professional or staff development, and development of appropriate staffing structures supportive of the student affairs' vision.

12.	I understand the organizational structure of my division.	0 1 2 3 n/a
13.	I am comfortable guiding staff with the creation of professional development plans.	0 1 2 3 n/a
14.	I am knowledgeable about the organizational structure of the institution.	0 1 2 3 n/a
15.	I collaborate with the VPSA regularly on staffing and organizational issues.	0 1 2 3 n/a
16.	I am comfortable creating structures within an organization.	0 1 2 3 n/a
17.	I am comfortable holding staff accountable for its performance.	0 1 2 3 n/a
18.	I can identify staff strengths and create strong teams.	0 1 2 3 n/a

Leadership and Strategic Vision: Understanding full culture and environment of the institution, the role student affairs plays within the environment, change management, and the long-term direction of student affairs.

19.	I am familiar with the divisional and institutional mission, vision, and goals.	0 1 2 3 n/a
20.	I have read and am familiar with annual reports and other documents related to divisional effectiveness.	0 1 2 3 n/a
21.	I have a fundamental understanding of the culture of my institution.	0 1 2 3 n/a
22.	I can develop a plan to evaluate and lead units and organizations through change.	0 1 2 3 n/a
23.	I can make effective and appropriate choices when faced with competing priorities.	0 1 2 3 n/a
24.	I can advocate effectively the institution's priorities at external events and with different constituencies.	0 1 2 3 n/a
25.	I understand the long-term direction of the division and how this direction aligns with the institutional vision and mission.	0 1 2 3 n/a

Resource Allocation, Acquisition, and Management: Continually identifying ways to attract, align, and maximize resources within the division.

26.	I understand the basic principles of budget management.	0 1 2 3 n/a
27.	I can identify key collaborators necessary for resource acquisition.	0 1 2 3 n/a

AVP Self-Assessment

28. I can write a grant application, or know to whom to go for this service.	0	1	2	3	n/a
29. I am comfortable with fundraising and have made "the Ask" for divisional programs.	0	1	2	3	n/a
30. I understand the university budgeting process.	0	1	2	3	n/a
31. I can successfully engage leadership in resource allocation discussions.	0	1	2	3	n/a
32. I understand the different types of resources available to me at my institution.	0	1	2	3	n/a

Strategic Assessment and Evaluation: Understanding the development of outcomes, creating and implementing assessment protocols, and interpreting data for long-range planning.

33. I know the learning outcomes associated with my areas of oversight.	0	1	2	3	n/a
34. I can develop learning outcomes.	0	1	2	3	n/a
35. I successfully use assessment data to advance divisional priorities.	0	1	2	3	n/a
36. I have developed an effective divisional assessment plan.	0	1	2	3	n/a
37. I understand how assessment data can be used to "tell the student affairs story."	0	1	2	3	n/a
38. I can link data to key goals and objectives for the division.	0	1	2	3	n/a
39. I understand how student affairs learning outcomes connect with the institutional strategic plan.	0	1	2	3	n/a

Law and Policy: Understanding the most current public policy, legislative changes, and legal decisions that affect higher education and developing student affairs practices that adhere to policy and law.

40. I have a fundamental understanding of federal laws including ADA, FERPA, Title IX, VAWA, and HIPAA.	0	1	2	3	n/a
41. I can articulate how law and policy affect the work of my areas of supervision.	0	1	2	3	n/a
42. I engage my staff in law and policy changes on a regular basis.	0	1	2	3	n/a
43. I can articulate how changes in law and policy that affect student affairs also affect the institution.	0	1	2	3	n/a
44. I am comfortable discussing issues of concern with the university's general counsel.	0	1	2	3	n/a
45. I know the role student affairs plays in compliance with key laws.	0	1	2	3	n/a
46. I regularly read about policy and law issues in higher education.	0	1	2	3	n/a

Note. The AVP Self-Assessment was created by Julie Payne-Kirchmeier on behalf of NASPA's AVP Steering Committee (2015).

Appendix C

AVP Productivity Planner

M T W T F S S

DATE:

WORD OF THE DAY:

THINGS THAT MUST GET DONE TODAY:

PRIORITIES:

STRATEGIC GOALS
The biggest initiatives I must keep moving forward

#1:	#2:	#3:

RELATIONSHIPS | SELF-CARE

People I must reach out to today to build/strengthen a relationship | *What will you do for yourself today?*

Index

Figures and tables are indicated by f and t following the page number.

A

Academic affairs, 178–179, 188, 203
Activity fees, 125–126
Administrative assistants, 26, 32
Administrators. *See also* Vice president for student affairs (VPSA)
   governance structure and, 58–59. *See also* Organizational structure
   role of AVPs defined by, 39
Advanced degrees, 177, 191–194, 196–197, 204–205
Advancement opportunities, 158–160, 175–205
Advice for new AVPs, 31–32
Alfred, R., 120
Amenities, 17
American Association of University Professors (AAUP), 139
American College Personnel Association (ACPA), 5, 61, 92
American Council on Education (ACE), 120
Appleton, J. R., 80
Assessments and evaluations, 9, 30, 100–101. *See also* Self-assessment
Assistant vs. associate vice presidents, 41
Associate/assistant vice president (AVP) position. *See also* Role of AVPs
   advice for, 31–32
   beginning in. *See* First year as AVP
   budget for, 15
   career development, 158–160, 175–205
   deans in, 45–46, 103
   expectations for, 10–11, 31–32, 96–97, 107–108

   financial management and budgeting, 119–135. *See also* Fiscal resource management
   human resource management, 91–118. *See also* Human resource management
   relationship with VPSA. *See* Vice president for student affairs
   single vs. multiple AVP models, 37–48
   strategic vision and planning, 57–77. *See also* Strategic planning and vision
   supervision aspects of, 102–116. *See also* Supervisory aspects of AVP positions
   work–life balance, 137–154. *See also* Work–life balance
Atkins, K., 62, 75
Automation of tasks, 141–142
Autonomy, 47–48
Auxiliary units, 126–127, 129–130
AVP Steering Committee of NASPA, 5, 9–10

B

Balance in role of AVPs, 26–29, 43–45, 76
Balance in work–life, 137–154. *See also* Work–life balance
Banks, Willie, 106, 114
Banning, J. H., 52
Bardwick, J., 157, 161
Barr, M., 127
Beginning as AVP. *See* First year as AVP
Bender, B. E., 163
Benefits, 17
Bennett, N., 98
Bernard, J. M., 100
Berry, J. K., 67

Best practices, 48–51
Birnbaum, R., 82
Bogue, E. G., 83
Bolman, L, 51–53
Brinckerhoff, P., 122, 134
Bryan, H. A., 172
Bryson, J., 122
Budgets
    AVP competency and. *See* Fiscal resource management
    for AVP position, 15
    cuts to, 120
    development cycle of, 130–131
    formula-based budgeting, 128–129
    incremental budgeting, 128
    process for, 122–123
    responsibility-centered management, 129–130
    zero-based budgeting, 127
Burke, Peggy, 109
Burn out, 44
Business analysis, 131–134, 133*t*

C

Cabellon, E., 85
Campus culture, 51
Campus resources for professional development, 30
Career development
    of AVPs, 158–160, 175–205
    mentors and, 15–16, 178–179, 201, 204
    of staff members, 49, 112–113
Career plateaus, 158, 161
Change management, 47–48, 121, 145
Checklist for Success, 207–208
Cherrey, C., 75–76
Chief financial officers (CFOs), 130
Chief student affairs officers (CSAOs). *See* Vice president for student affairs (VPSA)
The Chronicle of Higher Education's job board, 97
Churchill, Winston, 36
Clark, E. C., 75–76
Clarke, S., 131–132
Clery Act, 166
Coercive power, 68, 111
Cognitive development, 150
Cognitive domain, work–life balance and, 150
Coleman, Karen Warren, xiii–xiv
Collaboration, 49, 72, 84
Colleagues. *See* Peers
College and University Professional Association for Human Resources, 16
Collins, K., 158–159
Communication
    conflict management and, 82–85
    maintaining, 50
    management skills and, 23–25
    organizational culture and, 23–24
    organizational structure and, 5
    position skills and, 7
    report structure and, 20
    sensitive information and, 109–110
    with staff members, 24–25, 64–65, 108–110, 115–116
    VASAs expectations and, 11, 44, 69–70, 107–108
Community colleges, 37
Compassion, 84
Competencies. *See* Professional competencies
Competition, 83, 106
Complaints, 23
Compliance issues, 167
Conferences, 30, 172
Conflict, 82–85
Confrontation, 84
Content career plateaus, 158
Context experts, 22
Continuing education, 29–30, 33, 165–168, 204–205. *See also specific degrees*
Cook, Les, 176, 185–190
Cooperation, 49, 72, 84
Core values, 193, 202, 204
Cost of living, 17
Covey, Steven, 141
Coworkers. *See* Peers
Creamer, D. G., 35, 53, 58, 93, 104–105
Credentials, 204–205. *See also specific degrees*

Credit for success, 71
Crimmin, Nancy, 57
Cross-functional experience, 188, 203
Culture, 51. *See also* Organizational culture

D

Dawson, J. B., 100
Day-to-day responsibilities
    balance with strategic initiatives, 8, 14, 26–29, 63–64, 76, 140
    fiscal management and, 134
    managing, 23, 32, 43–45
Deal, T., 51–53
Deans, AVPs as, 45–46, 103
de la Teja, Magdalena, 177, 195–198
Delegation of tasks, 44, 142, 144
Departments
    equity among, 45
    initial review of, 21–22
Developmental models of supervision, 99
Direct reports. *See* Staff members
Discrimination model, 100
Diversity of staff, 99
Dobrowski, Pauline, 57
Doctorate degrees, 191–194, 204–205
Domestic violence, 166
Donar funds, 126
Douglas, Doug, 148
Dual roles of AVPs, 45–46, 103
Dungy, G. J., 39
Dunkel, Norb, 110–111, 114, 116
Dyer, J. H., 94

E

Elimination of tasks, 141
Ellett, Tom, 113
Ellis, H., 80, 171
E-mail, 148
Emotional domain, work–life balance and, 151
Emotional intelligence (EI), 151
Employment
    advancement opportunities, 158–160, 175–205
    APV–VPSA relationship and, 66–67
    firm-run employee searches, 15–16
    interviews for, 14–16
    promotions, 158–160, 175–205
    references for, 14–15
    satisfaction with, 140, 171
    staff member career development, 49, 112–113
Enrollment management, 124, 128
Environment, knowledge of, 86–87, 122–123, 204
Ethics, politics and, 80
Evaluations, 9, 100–101. *See also* Self-assessment
Evans, D., 67
Expectations
    for AVPs, 10–11, 31–32, 96–97, 107–108
    supervision role and, 104–105, 110–111
Expertise, establishing, 50
Expert power, 67–68, 111

F

Faculty, 73. *See also* Academic affairs
Federal requirements, 9–10
Fees, academic, 125–126
Ferguson, Kimberly M., 106, 114
Fiduciary responsibility, 125–126
Financial resources. *See* Fiscal resource management
Financial statements, 125, 133–134, 133*t*
Firm-run employee searches, 15–16
First year as AVP, 13–33
    balance between roles of, 26–29
    Checklist for Success, 207–208
    first 90 days, 20–22
    interviews, 14–16
    management, up and down, 24–26
    offer, responding to, 16–17
    organizational fit, 18–19
    professional development, 29–30
    wisdom from VPSAs, 31–32
Fiscal resource management, 119–135
    auxiliary units, 126–127
    as AVP competency, 9
    budget development cycle, 130–131
    budget process, 122–123

business analysis, 131–134, 133*t*
fees, 125–126
formula-based budgeting, 128–129
fundraising, 126
government appropriations, 124
incremental budgeting, 128
resource allocation, acquisition, and management competency, 9
resource scarcity, 83
responsibility-centered management, 129–130
tuition, 124
understanding, 22, 25
zero-based budgeting, 127
Fit, organizational. *See* Organizational fit
Flat organizational structures, 46–47
Formula-based budgeting, 128–129
401(k) programs, 17
Freedom of Information Act, 15
French, J., 67, 111
Friedman, S., 139, 140
Functional areas, 113–114
Funding sources, 123–127
Fundraising, 126

G

Gallup's StrengthsFinder, 84–85, 146
Gender
    career advancement and, 158–159
    student issues and, 166
GI Bill, 138
Ginsberg, B., 39
Goals, 21–22, 69. *See also* Strategic planning and vision
Goldsmith, M., 2–4, 147
Goleman, D., 151
Gonzalez, Anna, 176, 190–194
Governance structure. *See* Organizational structure
Government appropriations, 124, 128
Grants, 9, 124

H

Hands, Ashanti, 35, 85–86
Hatch, N. W., 94
Hecht, Amy, xiii–xv, 1, 85–86, 119

Heffernan, E. T., 61
Hemphill, B. O., 162, 164
Hernandez, Cynthia, 96, 106, 109–110, 113, 155
Herrick, C. D., 93–94
Hierarchy organizational structure, 44–45, 58–59, 158
Higher education issues, 166–167
Hirt, J., 159
Home life. *See* Work–life balance
Housing programs, 129–130
Hughes, C., 161
Human capital, 164–165. *See also* Staff members
Human resource management, 91–118
    as AVP competency, 8, 52–53
    AVP supervision and management tips, 102–116
    multiple AVP structure success, 47–48
    supervision and management, 94–95
    supervision challenges, 95–98
    supervision models, 98–101
    supervision overview, 93–94
Humphrey, J., 67
Huy, Q. H., 60
Hytner, R., 60

I

Incremental budgeting, 128
Industry knowledge, 113–114
Informational power, 112
Information overload, 25–26
Innovative practices, 52, 55
Institution types
    campus culture and, 51
    organizational structure and, 36–37
    tuition and fee differences, 124–125
    work life differences based on, 159
Intangible resources, 120–121
Integrated development model (IDM), 99–100
Interim VPSAs, 170
Interviews for employment, 14–16

J

Jacquette, O., 120
Jobs. *See* Employment
Job satisfaction, 140, 171
Johnson, Levester, 175
Johnsrud, L. K., 169

K

Kadushin, A., 100, 105
Keeling, R., 62–63
Kindle, Joan L., 175
Klawitter, M., 87
Kloppenberg, L. A., 63, 72, 75
Klotz, Ann Marie, 13–14, 19, 27–28, 85
Komives, S., 172
Kotler, P., 63
Kuk, L., 36–37, 52, 54

L

Law and policy, 9–10
Law degrees, 196–197
Leadership
    adaptation ability and, 2
    competency of, 61–62
    defined, 58–59
    delegation of tasks and, 142
    human resources and, 8. *See also* Human resource management
    management and, 7–8, 75–76, 156
    from middle position, 59–61, 156
    power dynamics and, 67–68
    professional associations and, 172
    strategic vision and planning and, 8–9, 57–77. *See also* Strategic planning and vision
    transactional flaws and, 2–3, 3–4*t*
Leadership Exchange magazine, xiv
LeBanc, Brandi Hephner, xiii–xiv
Lee, K. L., 112
Legitimate power, 67, 112
Levinson, H., 67
Life balance. *See* Work–life balance
Life path, constructing, 149–150
Listening skills, 44, 49, 105–106, 194
Low, G. T., 112
Loyalty, 68–69

M

Management skills
    AVP-specific aspects, 102–116
    communication and, 23–26
    defined, 94
    initial review of service units, 21–22
    leadership and, 7–8, 75–76, 156
    for middle positions, 59–61
    supervision and, 94–95
Master's degrees, 177
Mastrodicasa, Jeanna, 79
Maxwell, Dan, 109
McCaffery, P., 80–82
Meetings, 27–28, 49, 115
Mentors
    AVPs as, 142, 172
    best practices and, 48
    career advancement and, 15–16, 178–179, 201, 204
Mian, A., 127, 131
Michael, Kelly Wesener, xiii–xiv
Middle management, 59–64, 76
Miles, S. A., 98
Mills, D. B., 63–64
Mission-focused approach, 106, 108–109. *See also* Strategic planning and vision
Mission statements, 83
Models of supervision, 98–101
Money management. *See* Fiscal resource management
Montez, J. M., 96
Moon, J., 80, 171
Morgan, G., 80, 82–83
Morrill Act, 138
Motivation, 156–157, 162–165
Motivational domain, work–life balance and, 152–153
Mullendore, R., 172
Multiple AVP models
    challenges, 45–46
    single AVP models vs., 37–42
    successes, 47–48
Murphy, P. E., 63
Myers-Briggs Type Indicator, 84–85

N

National Association of Student Personnel Administrators (NASPA)
  AVP Institute on resource management, 120
  AVP Steering Committee, 5, 9–10, 167–168
  Leadership Exchange magazine, xiv
  professional competencies, 61
  Professional Competency Areas for Student Affairs Practitioners, 5, 92
Negotiation, job interviews and, 14–16
Networking, 48, 172–173. *See also* Mentors; Support networks
"No," when to say, 28, 141, 194
Nominations for firm-run employee searches, 16
Northhouse, P. G., 58
"Not alone: The first report of the White House Task Force to Protect Students from Sexual Assault," 166
Nunez, W. J., 62

O

Offers for employment, 16–17
Office for Civil Rights, 166
Open-forum interview, 15
Organizational career plateaus, 158
Organizational culture
  career advancement and, 204
  communication and, 23–24
  self-assessment and, 85
  supervision, implications for, 105
  transactional flaws and, 4
  VPSA role and, 10
Organizational fit, 18–19, 159, 186–188, 204
Organizational politics, 79–89
  AVP competencies and, 6–7, 22
  AVP role and, 40–41, 55
  case study, 87–88
  conflict and, 82–85
  higher education and, 80–81, 81*f*
  political map, 81, 81*f*
  power and, 82
  success and, 85–87
Organizational structure, 35–56
  best practices, 48–51
  communication and, 5
  function of, 36–37
  hierarchy of, 44–45, 58–59, 158
  innovative directions and, 51–53
  organizational charts vs., 35–36
  politics and, 80–81, 81*f*. *See also* Organizational politics
  single vs. multiple AVP models, 37–48
Organizational values, 83

P

Payne-Kirchmeier, Julie, xv, 91
Peers
  multiple AVP structure success and, 47
  professional networking and, 48
  reviews from, 30
  single AVP structures and, 42
  as support network, 204
Pendakur, Vijay, 13–16, 19, 95, 102–103, 112–113
Performance appraisals, 100–101
Personal career plateaus, 158
Personal life. *See* Work–life balance
Personal needs, 26
Peska, Scott, 103, 106, 114
Petrosko, J., 62
Philosophy of supervision, 103–104
Physical domain, work–life balance and, 152
Piaget, Jean, 150
Pina, Jason B., 85–86, 119, 137
Politics. *See* Organizational politics
Portfolio of units, reviewing, 21–22
Position skills, 7
Power dynamics, 67–68, 82, 111–112
Priorities
  budgeting and, 130
  in first 90 days, 21–22
  information overload and, 25–26
  multiple-AVP structures and, 46
  single-AVP structures and, 44
  supervision and, 96–97
  work–life balance and, 42–43, 143–145
Private institutions, 124–125

Procrastination, 142–143
Productivity Planner worksheet, 213
Professional associations, 167, 172–173, 188–189, 204
Professional competencies, 5–10, 6t, 38–39, 52–53, 61–62. *See also* Leadership
Professional Competency Areas for Student Affairs Practitioners (ACPA & NASPA), 5, 92
Professional development, 29–30, 33, 167–168, 172–173
Professional fit. *See* Organizational fit
Professional level, 29–30
Professional networking, 48
Professional niche, 203–204
Pro forma financial statements, 125, 133–134, 133t
Promotions, 158–160, 175–205
Psychotherapy-based models of supervision, 99
Public institutions, 124–125

R

Raven, B., 67, 111–112
References for employment, 14–15
Referent power, 68, 111–112
Reflection, weekly, 31
Reinemund, Steven, 98
Reisser, L., 66, 79
Reiter, M., 2–4, 147
Relationship maturity, 71
Relationships
    with administrative assistants, 26
    AVP–VSPA, 65–71, 74–76
    best practices for, 48
    during first year as AVP, 31–32
    leadership and, 58, 65–71
    multiple AVP structure success and, 47
    partnership building, 171
    politics, AVP competencies and, 6–7
    productivity and, 147
    with staff members, 70–71, 102–103, 110, 115–116
    strategic planning process and, 71–74
Relocation compensation, 17
Report structure, 20

Resiliency, work–life balance, 150
Resource management. *See* Fiscal resource management
Responsibility-centered management, 129–130
Retirement programs, 17
Review of service units, 21–22
Reward power, 67, 111
Risk-taking, career advancement and, 190, 203
Role models, 42–43
Role of AVPs, 155–174
    ambiguity of, 96–97
    balancing, 26–29, 43–44, 76
    changes in, 169–170
    competencies, 5–10, 6t, 38–39, 52–53, 61–62
    dual, 45–46, 103
    effectiveness of, 161
    focus areas for, 162
    as interim VPSAs, 170
    leadership and. *See* Leadership
    maximizing, 168–169
    motivation and, 156–157, 162–165
    multiple AVP structures and, 40
    organizational structure and, 44–45
    overview of, 54–55
    partnership building, 171
    priorities for, 19
    professional development and, 172–173
    remaining in, reasons for, 157–161
    strategic planning and, 57–77. *See also* Strategic planning and vision
    transactional flaws and, 2–3, 3–4t
    VPSA's expectations and, 107–108
    work–life balance and, 139–140. *See also* Work–life balance
Role of VPSAs, 1–2, 42, 160, 194
Roper, L. D., 66, 68, 71, 79
Ross, Frank, 176–180
Rosser, V. J., 171

S

Salaries, 16–17
Sanford, N., 100
Scarcity of resources, 83

Scenario planning, 131
Second-level staff, 116
Self-assessment
　conflict resolution and, 84–85
　strengths, identifying, 104
　tool for, 209–211
　transactional flaws and, 4
　work–life balance, 146–149
Self-care, 145. *See also* Work–life balance
Self-directed learning, 29–30
Service fees, 125–126
Service units, reviewing, 21–22
Sexual assault, 166
Sexual orientation, 202
Shared visions, 63–64
Shults, C., 120
Sinek, S., 152–153
Single AVP models
　challenges, 42–45
　multiple AVP models vs., 37–42
　successes, 46–47
Six Guiding Behaviors and Guiding Questions (Stanley), 143
Skills. *See* Professional competencies
Social domain, work–life balance and, 151
Social media, 148–149
Spiritual domain, work–life balance and, 151
Sponsler, B. A., 63
Staff members. *See also* Human resource management; Supervisory aspects of AVP positions
　career development of, 49, 112–113
　communication with, 24–25, 64–65, 108–110, 115–116
　diversity of, 99
　empowering, 114–116, 165
　expectations for, 104–105
　initial review of, 21–22
　lack of, 44
　relationships with, 70–71, 102–103, 110, 115–116
　strategic vision and, 64–65, 108–110
　strengths of, 112–113
　successes of, recognizing, 115–116
　support and development of, 164–165
　talent development of, 29
Stakeholders
　politics and, 80–81, 81*f*

politics, AVP competencies and, 6–7
　strategic vision and, 20–21, 95–96
Stalking, 166
Stallings, Sean, 119
Stanley, Andy, 143
State aid, 124, 128
State requirements, 9–10
Stettler, Lori, 97
Stoltenberg, C., 99–100
Strategic planning and vision, 57–77
　AVP role and, 8–9
　balancing with day-to-day activities, 26–29
　budgeting for, 131–132
　competencies for, 61–62
　defined, 62–63
　leadership and, 58–59
　leading from middle position, 59–61
　management and, 74–76
　relationship management, 65–74
　resource allocation and, 121
　shared vision for, 63–65
　staff members, communicating to, 64–65, 108–110
　supervision and, 94–95
　understanding, 22
Strengths, identifying, 104, 112–113
Stress, 39, 55, 152. *See also* Work–life balance
Strickland, S., 120
Stringer, J., 81
Structural career plateaus, 158
Structure. *See* Organizational structure
Students
　impacts on, motivation and, 162–164
　issues relevant to, 166–167
　perspectives of, strategic planning and, 73–74
　social media and, 149
Success
　checklist for, 207–208
　credit for, 71
　organizational politics and, 85–87
　of staff members, 115–116
Supervisory aspects of AVP positions, 102–116
　challenges in, 95–98
　defined, 93–94

management and, 94–95
models of, 98–101
Support networks, 48, 188–189, 192, 204. *See also* Mentors
SWOT (strengths, weaknesses, opportunities, threats) analysis, 122–123
Synergistic models of supervision, 100–101

T

Taylor, C. M., 75
Teamwork
    management skills and, 7
    single-AVP structure and, 47
    strategic planning and, 71–73
Technology use, 148–149
Time management
    administrative assistants and, 32
    AVP Productivity Planner worksheet, 213
    "no," when to say, 28, 141, 194
    single-AVP structures and, 44
    strategies for, 27–28
    work–life balance and, 140–143
Transactional flaws, 2–3, 3–4t, 147
Transition or turbulent periods, 39, 55
Transparency, 50, 70
Truman, Harry, 71
Trust
    best practices for, 48
    relationship management and, 67–70
    in supervision, 101
    between VPSAs and AVPs, 11, 21
Tuition, 124

U

Unit directors, AVPs as, 45–46, 103
Unit managed budgets, 129–130

V

Vaden, R., 141–143
Values
    organizational, 83
    personal, 193, 202, 204
Vice president for student affairs (VPSA)
    budget development cycle and, 130–131
    communicating with, 23–25, 50, 69
    expectations for AVPs, 10–11, 31–32, 44, 107–108
    politics, AVP competencies and, 6–7
    promotion to, personal stories, 175–205
    relationship with AVPs, 65–71, 74–76
    role of, 1–2, 42, 160, 194
    strategic planning and, 63
    trust of AVPs and, 11, 21, 67–70
    work–life balance and, 194
Violence Against Women Reauthorization Act (2013), 166
Vision. *See* Strategic planning and vision

W

Ward-Roof, Jeanine A., 35
Welsh, J. F., 62
Wesaw, A. J., 63
Westfall, Sarah, 177, 198–202
What Got You Here, Won't Get You There (Goldsmith & Reiter), 2
White House report on sexual violence, 166
White, Lori, 176, 180–184
Whitney, R., 73
Winston, R. B., 35, 53, 58, 93, 104–105
Work–life balance, 137–154
    AVP role and, 139–140
    cognitive domain and, 150
    emotional domain and, 151
    guiding questions for, 145–149
    historical context for, 138–139
    life path, constructing, 149–150
    motivational domain and, 152–153
    physical domain and, 152
    prioritizing and, 143–145
    resiliency and, 150
    single-AVP structure and, 42–43
    social domain and, 151
    spiritual domain and, 151
    time management and, 140–143
    VPSA role and, 194
Work overload, 28, 42–43

Y
Young, R. B., 163
Young, Wayne, Jr., 96, 106

Z
Zero-based budgeting, 127